FOUNDATIONAL BLACK AMERICAN RACE BAITER

FOUNDATIONAL BLACK AMERICAN RACE BAITER

My Journey into Understanding
Systematic Racism

By
TARIQ NASHEED

FOUNDATIONAL BLACK AMERICAN RACE BAITER

My Journey Into Understanding Systematic Racism

KING FLEX
ENTERTAINMENT

Dedicated to the Nasheed family, Alexis Nasheed, Taria Nasheed, TJ Nasheed, Asir Nasheed, Mateo Nasheed, and Shirley Rayford. Also a special blessing goes out to the master teachers who I and so many others have learned from: The late Dr. Frances Cress Welsing, Neely Fuller Jr., Shahrazad Ali, Dr. Kaba Kamene, Professor James Small, Dr. Phil Valentine, Anthony T. Browder, and Dr. Claud Anderson.

CONTENTS

INTRODUCTION   1

CHAPTER ONE: Understanding Racism As A Child   7

CHAPTER TWO: Why Racial Equality is Seen as Unfair   19

CHAPTER THREE: The Religion of White Supremacy   27

CHAPTER FOUR: Common Misconceptions About White Supremacy   41

CHAPTER FIVE: Race and Relationships   57

CHAPTER SIX: Racial Politics In The Workplace   79

CHAPTER SEVEN: Perceived Allies   121

CHAPTER EIGHT: The "I'm White And I Say So" Rule   161

CHAPTER NINE: Common Deception Tactics of White Supremacy   191

CHAPTER TEN: Strategies Black People Can Use To Produce Justice   209

SUMMARY   227

REFERENCE LIST   231

INTRODUCTION

I really don't like to give myself specific titles. Whenever I do television or radio interviews, hosts always ask me under what title would I like to be referred. The only exception is when I sometimes appear on Fox News, and they take it upon themselves to give me some bogus title that they made up like "Black Lives Matter leader". They do this to dog whistle to their anti-Black viewership, to know that I'm supposed to be perceived as the enemy.

So I go in knowing they have an agenda.

But my title generally changes depending on the project I'm promoting at the moment. If I'm promoting a book, my title is author. If I'm promoting one of my documentary films, my title is filmmaker or director. If I'm promoting a music project or iPhone app, my title will be amended to reflect that.

Because I speak out against anti-Black racism on a daily basis on my social media sites, and I have had a lot of input in many justice movements around the world, most mainstream media outlets give me the title of activist.

I have been skeptical of wearing that title as well, because all victims of racism should be activists. That title should not be relegated to a select few in Black society. Black empowerment has to be a group phenomenon – because systematic white supremacy is maintained through a group effort. It's a team sport.

So the most apt title that I could give myself is anti-racism strategist. I'm simply one person who is trying to come up with strategies for how to dismantle the system of racism.

Another title I prefer is Foundational Black American. This is a descriptive term that identifies non-immigrant, native Black Americans who are primarily descended from enslaved people in North America. We are a very unique and distinct ethnic group because we descended from the people who were literally the foundation of the United States of America.

Other ethnic groups, including many African and Caribbean groups, go out of their way to distinguish themselves from us. There are festivities and celebrations held in the United States like the Puerto Rican Day Parade, the Jamaican Day Carnival, Cinco De Mayo, the West Indian Parade, etc., where people get together and celebrate the history and uniqueness of their distinct ethnic group and culture. Black Americans have always respected these cultures and these celebrations, and other ethnic groups should show the same respect to Foundational Black Americans who recognize, celebrate and advocate for our own distinct ethnic group.

Foundational Black Americans have fought for the right of other groups to come to our ancestral homeland and enjoy all the tangible benefits. In the process, often times we have neglected to make sure our own ethnic and cultural group has the proper energy and resources to fight against the constant onslaught of systematic white supremacy.

The concept of groups of people being mistreated because they were born the wrong color, according to the rules of another oppressive group, has never sat right with my spirit.

I can't speak for anyone else, but I know for a fact that I was not put on this planet by the Creator to accept being subordinate to another group based on race. To me, the thought of accepting racial non-justice has always seemed disrespectful to God.

So I have always felt a desire and obligation come up with ways to try to figure out how to replace the system of racism with a system of justice, as articulated by author Neely Fuller JR.

Many people in the dominant society have labeled me as a race baiter. In fact, when you google the term "race baiter," at one point my name and picture was literally the first thing that showed up in the search.

Generally, the term race baiter is used by suspected white supremacists to try to deflect criticism of their own racist views.

In the current context in which the term is used, I have found that no one seems able to give a logical definition of what a race baiter, or race baiting, is. One definition in Merriam Webster's dictionary defines race baiting as "the making of verbal attacks against members of a racial group." Many Black people are labeled race baiters for merely pointing out instances of systematic racism, so this definition isn't applicable.

Some people have also defined race baiting as falsely claiming a situation is racial when racial bias is not a factor. This definition is also problematic because systematic white supremacy dominates every part of our society.

There is no area of activity that is devoid of systematic white supremacist domination. So that definition also strikes me as illogical. The fact that no one seems able to offer a logical definition as to what a race baiter is leads me to assume that the term is a coded epithet.

Similar to the word nigger.

Contrary to popular belief, there is also no logical definition for the word nigger. Some dictionaries define it as an "ignorant person" and most dictionaries generally define it as "a derogatory term for a Black person."

If the word nigger meant "ignorant person", why aren't other racial groups of ignorant people called nigger? That definition makes no sense. And if the word nigger means a derogatory word for Black people, why is the term derogatory?

As author Neely Fuller Jr. has pointed out, this is the reason why the word has been so effective: because no one can give a reason for why the word nigger is derogatory or negative.

And the open-ended connotation of the word has made it hard to counter because no one knows, exactly, what they are being called when the word nigger is hurled at them.

Mr. Fuller has given the word a compensatory definition. He has correctly concluded that the word nigger simply means "victim of white supremacy."

I have taken a similar stance with the term race baiter. Since the people who wield that term against Black people generally cannot logically define it, I have given it a compensatory definition. A race baiter is a person who points out certain layers of systematic racism and baits suspected white supremacists into revealing themselves.

By using this definition, I am 100% a race baiter. Systematic white supremacy is the main issue that affects the lives of non-white people globally, and I have been on a lifelong mission trying to figure out a solution to the question of how to replace this system of white supremacy - which is the most powerful system on the planet - with a system of justice.

CHAPTER ONE

Understanding Racism
As A Child

I spent the first few years of my life in Detroit. Detroit has always been a center for prominent social, religious, musical and revolutionary movements. The Nation of Islam was founded in Detroit. The legendary Motown sound and the Parliament Funkadelic movement both originated out of Detroit. Malcolm X was known as Detroit Red because of the city's impact on him. One of the early pioneers of contemporary street literature, Donald Goines, came out of Detroit.

As a small child living in Detroit in the 1970s, the energy from all these significant cultural movements suffused the atmosphere of the city. And early on I absorbed that energy. I carry that same energy today, which can be seen in my urban themed books and my socially conscious documentary films.

I was one of those weird kids who wasn't afraid of anything. I think this probably had less to do with having courage, and more to do with not understanding the concept of danger at the time. And for a child who's three or four-years-old, that's not always a good thing.

I would do things like climb on the roof of the house and jump off while doing a flip. At four-years-old, I would often sneak into my mother's car and try to drive off. Back in the 70s, many cars didn't need a key to put the vehicle in neutral or reverse. So, if I saw the car was unlocked, I would just hop in, throw the gear in reverse, and back the car out into the street. Thank goodness I never hit another car, and I somehow never got hurt.

Another thing I liked to do at that age was wander away from the house. On a couple of occasions when my mother was at work and I was being watched by a relative, I would casually leave the house and wander the streets of Detroit at four-years-old.

I would trek through the city, absorbing all the sights, smells, and sounds of this huge urban landscape. I would curiously observe a neighborhood full of beautiful Black people getting off buses from work, driving Cadillacs down the streets, and standing on the corners drinking, laughing, arguing, mingling with each other. I was fascinated by people and to this day I still have that fascination.

At that time, I was driven by this innate desire to explore beyond the parameters that were – correctly – set for me as a toddler. Luckily, I was never harmed during these spontaneous excursions through the city. Usually some concerned citizen would spot this four-year-old child wandering around by himself and would have the decency to take me down to a local police station, where my panicked mother would have already called in a missing child report. So I would always eventually make it home safe.

My mother felt it was time to make some changes. My mother and I shared a flat with my aunt and her two children. My aunt would watch after me when my mother went to work at her job at Michigan Bell. Sometimes when my mom and aunt were at work, I would stay at my uncle's house nearby. My dad would come around every blue moon, so he couldn't be relied on to help raise me.

At the time, my mother and my other adult family members were relatively young. They were all in their mid to late twenties, so they were partying, socializing, having cookouts and get-togethers on a frequent basis. Trying to keep eyes on a dangerously rambunctious kid like myself in this environment was challenging.

My mother decided to send me down to her hometown of Leeds, Alabama to stay with my grandmother. One of my uncles flew me down there, and soon after, my mother relocated to join me. She was able to transfer her job to another telecommunications company, South Central Bell, which was headquartered in Birmingham, Alabama. Eventually, I lived back and forth between Leeds and Birmingham, staying with my grandmother, who was older, retired and better suited to keeping an eye on me whenever my mother would rotate different shifts at her job.

I eventually settled in and enrolled in elementary school in Leeds. Leeds was a small town with a population of less than 8000 people at that time. The city had been partially founded by newly freed Foundation Black American former slaves a couple decades after the Civil War (Fraser, 1980; Wright, 1974). Many Black people gravitated there after slavery to work in the cement industry and the expanding railroad system. In fact, the legend of John Henry, the story of the Black railroad worker mythologized as the "steel driving man," who won a competition against a steam-powered rock drilling machine, is said to have originated out of Leeds (Garst, 2002).

Living in Leeds was a totally different experience than Detroit. There were no big Cadillacs driving around. No large buildings or skyscrapers. No music from Aretha Franklin, The Spinners, or Funkadelic bumping from people's windows. None of the groovy looking grown-ups hanging out on the corners, socializing in their slick clothes.

Now it was just huge backyards. A plethora of insect sounds. And the only music bumping was the AM gospel station my grandmother listened to every morning. Now my world consisted of watching the beautiful fireflies that would come out at night (many firefly species have since gone extinct and that's why we rarely see them today, but in the 70s they were everywhere in the South). I'm also surrounded by hilly roads and wooded areas. And, most interestingly, I'm having a completely new experience that I did not have in Detroit.

Being around white people.

This experience sparked the reshaping of my thought process that has continued throughout my life. Because these weren't just white people I was interacting with in school. Most of these people were – and this was by their own admission – white supremacists.

Up until the mid 1960s, white people who believed in open anti-Black racism were loud and proud about it. They wore white supremacy on their sleeves. They specifically used the words white supremacy to explain their ideology and culture.

Many of white America's forefathers used the term white supremacy in their writings and speeches. In his book, *Notes on The State of Virginia* (Jefferson, 1982), Thomas Jefferson went into great pseudo-scientific detail about how he believed Black people were inherently inferior to whites.

Abraham Lincoln also openly discussed how he felt Black people were inferior to whites. Many early white feminists like Susan B. Anthony, Elizabeth Cady Stanton, Belle Kearney and others also promoted the ideology of white supremacy (Etcheson, 2020; Perkins, 1981). One of the more prominent white feminist leaders, Carrie Chapman Catt, infamously said: "white supremacy will be strengthened, not weakened, by women's suffrage (Enoch, 2020; Sanghani, 2015)."

There were laws throughout the United States that openly enforced white supremacist doctrine. In particular, the 1857 Dred Scott Supreme Court ruling, for example, explicitly stated that Black people were *legally* inferior under the law (Benton, 1857; Higginbotham, 1978).

During the so-called Jim Crow era, there were dozens and dozens of popular books that promoted white supremacy, such as: *The Negro a Beast* by Charles R. Carroll, *The Passing of the Great Race* by Madison Grant, *The Rising Tide of Color Against White World-Supremacy* by Lothrop Stoddard, and many others.

There was also the Eugenics movement, which eventually spread to international societies, that manufactured a pseudo-scientific basis for white supremacist ideologies.

The point is, white supremacy was a term that the people who believed in white supremacy forced on their non-white victims. And, most importantly, all sectors of the dominant society used the term white supremacy and *openly* practiced it up through the late 1960s. After the Civil Rights laws of the mid-60s were enacted, legal penalties could be imposed on people or institutions that *openly* practiced systematic white supremacy. The dominant society had to learn how to continue to practice the same systematic white supremacy by using coded language.

It took a while for the white supremacists to adjust to using these codes. By the late 70s, many adult white supremacists had learned how to encrypt their racism.

But their children? Not so much.

When I started at Leeds Elementary School, many of the white students let me know they had been well-trained in anti-Black racism at an early age. And these kids had no filter or coded language. Their racial rhetoric was blatant.

During the 70s, "busing" was a big deal for schools around the country. In response to the 1960s desegregation laws, there was a nationwide practice of transporting students by bus to schools outside their local school districts to reduce the racial segregation in schools.

There was a lot of animosity and resentment on the part of white families and students, because they felt they were forced to go the same schools as Black children. Some white families around the country opted out of this perceived "forced" integration by sending their children to private schools or charter schools, if they had the resources. But many of the poor and working-class white families had no choice but to go along with the program and send their children to school with the "coloreds".

Consequently, the white kids at my school had to show their social "superiority" by constantly berating many of us Black students with racial taunts. And these were six-year-old white children we are talking about. I learned then that many children in the dominant society are taught the basics of systematic white supremacy at an early age. This fact remains true today.

If you take a listen to the chatter on modern online video games, you will be inundated with anonymous young white children screaming the word nigger in its full racist context.

Some of my white classmates at Leeds Elementary School would make up little racist rhymes and recite them in the lunchroom to antagonize us. "Blacks come from Jupiter, that's why they're stupider" is one rhyme I vividly remember.

I noticed that many of the other Black children didn't know how to react. Many were confused as to why they were being called names. For the most part, Black parents don't really teach Black children about systematic racism. Black children are taught, if they do experience racism, to try to ignore it and to thrive in spite of racism. Rarely do Black people discuss the basics of systematic racism, especially with their children.

My fellow Black classmates showed a generally passive disposition in response to the white children's racist taunts and rhetoric.

My reaction was different.

Having lived in Detroit just a short time before I enrolled at Leeds Elementary, I had absorbed a lot of the social atmosphere of the city. A lot of the energy from the Black Power movement was still flowing through the collective consciousness of Detroit. Some of my uncles even participated in the racial riot that happened a few years earlier in the city. The spirit of a no-nonsense type of Black pride still resonated in Detroit, as well as other major urban centers around the country.

Even though I did not understand the concept of racism at that time, I still carried the spirit of Black pride I had picked up through osmosis.

When I encountered the white supremacist rhetoric of my classmates in Leeds, Alabama, I instinctively knew that this was something I wasn't supposed to and didn't have to tolerate. As a result, I always pushed back against their racism. One reason I did this is because their racial views were illogical to me. These kids would always talk about how "poor" and inferior Black people were, but I reminded them that we all took the same bus to school together. That meant I knew where they lived and I knew what their homes looked like. In the Black area of Leeds where I lived with my grandmother, the neighborhood was a clean, working-class environment with modest but well-maintained homes. But in the area where many of these white supremacist students lived, their homes were dilapidated trailers and filthy shacks.

Many of the white supremacist students would come to school with dirty clothes and a lack of clean hygiene. Some of them would smell like they hadn't taken a bath in days.

Most of us Black children came to school sparking clean. At that time, Black families generally would not allow their children to leave the house in an unpresentable manner. If they allowed their children to walk out of the house filthy and unclean, Black parents felt that this would reflect badly on them.

Even at my young age, I knew the white kid's claims about how superior they were compared to Black children were completely illogical. And once I reminded them how filthy many of them were living, they would usually back off.

As the years went by, I learned all the ways in which white students had – and have – certain privileges over Black students. After Civil Rights legislation passed in the mid-60s, it became illegal to openly segregate schools based on race. In the 1970s, when forced integration was being implemented in schools around the country, white supremacists came up with new and novel ways to segregate Black children from white children.

One of these strategies was to implement different special education programs within school systems. Around the country many Black students were disproportionately funneled into learning and behavioral disability classes for completely arbitrary reasons.

The white children at my school couldn't read or write any better than most of the Black children, yet they were rarely placed in special education classes. But Black children were placed in these classes in large numbers. In fact, one of my white teachers tried to have me placed into a special education class for behavioral issues. Luckily my mother didn't sign off.

Another thing I noticed was that Black students were disproportionately disciplined or suspended, much more often than the white students. During this time, I learned one of the most important rules of systematic white supremacy:

White children don't get punished.

To this day, as a society we rarely see white children systematically punished for anything. Punishments for Black children, on the other hand, are always justified.

White children at my school would constantly disrupt class, fight, even call-in fake bomb threats to the school, yet they would still get preferential treatment from the school officials. At worst they would get a verbal reprimand.

But Black children were suspended, expelled, or placed in special classes for any minor infraction, real or imagined. One year, me and some white classmates who I became cool with were hanging out in the hallway before our next class. As a harmless prank, the white boys started hitting the lockers with their hands real loud in the hallway, then running off to class. Each kid did this one at a time and I wanted to get in on the fun, so I joined in. I hit one of the lockers and ran to my next class, laughing along with my classmates at how startled the other students in the hallway were.

Later that day I was called into the principal's office because of my participation in the prank. All the teachers, including the principal, and the other students knew that the white kids I was hanging out with were also banging on the lockers along with me. I was following *their* lead in the prank.

Yet I was the only one who was singled out. Not only was I verbally reprimanded by the principal, but he also informed me that I was *expelled* from school altogether for causing a disturbance.

Nothing happened to the white students.

This was a pivotal moment for me. A major and early wake-up call. It became crystal-clear that I, and other Black children, were being treated differently and unfairly based on our race. Like any child who is mistreated, I wanted to know why.

But none of the adults around me at the time could provide an answer. I couldn't get an answer from anyone in white society because one of the main rules for maintaining refined systematic white supremacy is to deny that it exists.

I could not get thorough answers from the people in my family. They would give general warnings about how I needed to be careful if I went into certain neighborhoods, or how I should watch my back around racist white kids at school.

But no one could explain to me why such an unfair system existed. And no one could tell me how to find protection from this cruel system.

So, at a young age, I decided to make it my life's mission to find those answers.

CHAPTER TWO

Why Racial Equality is Seen as Unfair

I remember the first school play in which I participated. I was around 7-years-old and I was assigned to play baseball legend Hank Aaron. I don't remember what the play was about because I was solely focused on my one line. All through the 1970s, Hank Aaron was a hot topic because he broke Babe Ruth's home run record. In my school play, a white kid played Babe Ruth and I had on a brand-new baseball outfit, with the cap and bat, ready to play Mr. Aaron in front of an auditorium full of parents and teachers.

I still remember my one little line verbatim after all these years. I walked up on stage, faced my little co-star, and said to him in a semi-nervous voice:

"Excuse me Mr. Ruth.... I broke your home run record... I like baseball too."

After I delivered my line, I could see all the Black parents in the audience, including my mother, giving me a grand round of applause. And I felt great about it. But the thing that really stood out to me was the reaction of the white parents in the audience, who gave me some lighthearted courtesy applause. But nothing like the Black parents. Some white parents almost had a look of disdain in their faces after my brief performance. For the life of me I couldn't figure out what their problem was. My little one liner in the play was definitely on par, or better than many of the other white students who got on stage and delivered their lines. I didn't really let it bother me too much at the time, but it was yet another experience that made me curious about racial attitudes.

Years later, when I was older, I would stumble on some information that explained why the white parents seemed so low-key hostile towards me after my performance. One of my favorite books growing up was the *Guinness Book of World Records*. I would check out each updated annual edition from my school's library on a regular basis. I would read them from front to back, entertaining myself learning random tidbits and stats.

One tidbit from the Guinness book really stood out to me one year. It listed the record for the most amount of mail sent to a private citizen in a single year. To my surprise, that record holder was Hank Aaron.

I did more research and found that suspected white supremacists around the country had sent Hank Aaron almost a million pieces of hate mail (Benson, 2009; Spencer, 2003), all because he broke Babe Ruth's home run record.

There has always been a lot of racial hostility towards Black athletes who broke certain color barriers or overturned records set by white players.

This explained why I received such weird energy from some of the white parents in the audience during my school play. The lesson I took away is that in a system of white supremacy, racial equality is deemed unfair.

In the collective psyche of white supremacists, they have to make sure a system is in place that deprives non-white people, and Black people in particular, of resources, protection, tangibles and opportunities. The only way they feel they can compete is when the odds are systematically stacked against Black people.

This is why they are so hyper-sensitive about sports. In sports, the success of participants results from their individual abilities. Based on the general rules of organized sports, participants cannot depend on systematic racial advantages and societal privileges to win.

In sports, everything is mono e mono. Man vs man, woman vs woman. Everything is generally based on equal abilities. Because things are set up to be equal in sports, Black people usually excel over their non/white counterparts. Without an unjust racial system to create obstacles for Black people, white supremacists view equality as unfair.

This is why, historically, many Black athletes have been systematically punished outside their chosen profession. This is especially true for Black boxers. Prize fighters from Jack Johnson to Muhammad Ali to Mike Tyson, all the way up to Floyd Mayweather, were criminalized by the dominant society.

The systematic punishment of Black athletes can be interpreted as the dominant society saying, "we can't beat you Black people in the ring, but we can beat you *outside* the ring, using our system of racism."

In the collective psyche of white supremacists, equal competition is viewed as unfair, while a system that creates racial obstacles and disadvantages for Black people is viewed as fair.

This racial dynamic plays out in every area of social activity. And whiteness itself is based on the systematic subjugation of Black people.

Systematic deprivation within Black society is the standard by which white supremacy is measured. For example, white supremacists feel society is equal and just when predominantly Black schools suffer from a lack of resources. When Black people started to advocate for equal resources for

Black schools - as was the initial intent of the infamous *Brown v. The Board of Education* case in the 1950s - the dominant society will often push back violently.

They believe everything is equal when policies are put in place to keep Black people from getting fair housing, employment, and economic opportunities. The objective is to socially engineer Black people to remain as a noncompetitive underclass.

When we observe the history of America, we will see that there has never been a systematic program or allocation of resources that *specifically* and exclusively benefitted Foundational Black Americans.

Specific resources have been allocated to Native Americans, Japanese Americans, and other ethnic groups through immigration programs. The whole Jim Crow era was nothing more than a nationwide affirmative action program for white people.

But Foundational Black Americans have never received any tangible benefits from the U.S. government *at the exclusion* of other groups. And the ironic thing is that white supremacists like to pretend that Black people are somehow accumulating a plethora of unearned benefits from the government.

This is a mass con game that anti-Black racists like to play in order to deflect from the truthful allocation of compensatory resources to Black society, which are rightfully deserved.

The dominant society likes to pretend that Black people are hoarding resources through programs like affirmative action and other "minority" set asides. Yet they are fully aware that the greatest beneficiaries of affirmative action are white women. Further, the term minority encompasses a myriad of ethnic, racial, religious, sexual and gender groups.

The dominant society also likes to perpetuate the myth of the Black welfare recipient. This degrading narrative of poor, hyper-sexualized Black women having as many children possible in order to "game the system" was solidified in the 1970s.

Starting in 1974, the American media started to circulate a story using the moniker "Welfare Queen" to describe the exploits of a woman named Linda Taylor (Gilman, 2013; Riches, 2017). Taylor was charged with committing large-scale welfare fraud by using four aliases. Born Martha Miller or, according to some sources Martha Louise White, the woman with a slightly dark complexion was able to pass as multiple different races and ethnicities such as Jewish, Black American, Asian or Puerto Rican.

During Ronald Reagan's 1976 presidential campaign, he sent racist dog whistles to his supporters during his speeches by making anecdotal references to a "Chicago woman" who had defrauded the government (Demby, 2013; Shaw, 1999) of thousands of dollars in food stamps and welfare. This was a propaganda technique that came to be known in political circles as the Southern Strategy. Politicians would gain support among white voters by appealing to their anti-Black racism by using coded language. So words like "Chicago" became synonymous with "Black" (this is still true today), and welfare mother or welfare queen because synonymous with single Black women.

The ironic thing about Linda Taylor becoming the template for the Black female welfare recipient stereotype is that Taylor was actually classified as white on her birth certificate and on her death certificate.

The Culture of "Case Pleading"

Living under a system of racial oppression has caused Black people to create a culture in which we are constantly pleading our case to the dominant society. Black people spend a considerable amount of time trying to convince white society that the racial injustices that we are subjected to exist. This has become a futile, energy wasting, non-productive subculture that Black people have created in reaction to systematic subjugation.

The dominant white society is fully aware of the racial oppression that Black people endure. They are the ones who created the system of white supremacy. When Black people try to plead their cases to the dominant society, many of us don't want to accept the simple fact that the majority of white society simply doesn't care. We think that if we can get white society to see how physically, emotionally, mentally, or economically downtrodden and broken we are, we will be able to appeal to some sympathetic sense of humanity they are presumed to possess.

We seem to forget that collectively the dominant white society never had a problem with Jim Crow, where anti-Black laws and policies were openly practiced. The dominant society never got together and said, "we need to stop all this racism against the negroes." It was the violent uprising of Black Americans in the 1960s that made society change these laws (at least on paper).

Nonetheless, many of these anti-Black policies are still practiced through codified common laws among white supremacists. White supremacists spent the last few centuries building a system of racial inequality where white people were on top and Black people were required to be positioned firmly on the bottom (with other racial buffer classes in between). Black people are going to have to accept that white supremacists are never going to dismantle an unequal and unjust racial system that they fought so hard to create.

It will be the task of white supremacy's victims to figure out how to replace the system of white supremacy with a system of justice.

CHAPTER THREE

The Religion of White Supremacy

In the early 80s, I went back and forth between two middle schools: Robert E. Lee Middle School (named after the white supremacist Confederate general) in Birmingham, Alabama and Leeds Middle School in Leeds, Alabama. Some years earlier the Leeds school had been named Moton High School after the Foundational Black American author and educator, Robert Russa Moton. When the school was called Moton, all the students were Black. In fact, my mother and all my aunts and uncles attended the school in the 1950s and 60s.

After desegregation laws were implemented in the 1970s, white teachers were brought in and white students were bussed into the Black neighborhood where school was located. This was done because the city didn't really have a budget at the time to build a middle school in the white neighborhood. Evidently, the white supremacists didn't want their children going to a school named after a Black man, so they changed the name of the school from Moton to Leeds Middle School.

Fast forward to today and there is a new Leeds Middle School built on the other side of town, and the old building in the Black area that was named Leeds Middle School is once again named Moton. Now it's called the Moton Community Center. After white students didn't have to attend the facility anymore, the city felt it was ok to name the building after a Black man again.

This was the casual, normalized, systematic white supremacist environment I grew up around when I lived in Leeds. It wasn't the stereotypical racism portrayed in movies where all the white supremacists are angry, aggressive psychopaths who are members of the Klan or skinheads. Even though a few of my white classmates would occasionally get verbally aggressive with their racism, I noticed that there was a calm, almost religious consistency to the racism that was practiced by most of the white people around me.

And instinctively, I knew something was incorrect about this "religion", even as a child.

On the morning of January 27th, 1983, the white woman who was my home room teacher at Leeds Middle School made a somber announcement. She announced that a well-known football coach in the state of Alabama, Coach Bear Bryant, had died the previous day. Paul "Bear" Bryant was a white man who was the head coach of the University of Alabama football team. White people in Alabama took this guy very seriously. If you went to a white person's home in Alabama during that time, you would often see a picture of fake white Jesus on the wall, and next to that would be a picture of Bear Bryant.

After my teacher announced Bear Bryant's death, she then told the class to bow our heads for a moment of silent prayer. We were all sitting there in class, silently praying, and I'll never forget how dumb I felt. I was thinking to myself, "I'm really sitting here praying over a damn football coach, who I honestly care nothing about."

This was the same school that miseducated me about almost everything related to Black history. Every Black historical figure they taught us about came with a negative connotation. For example, I didn't learn about the greatness of Marcus Garvey until I was an adult. As a child in school, I remember being taught that Garvey was a Black radical who went to jail for fraud because of his Back-to-Africa scheme.

I also noticed that whenever we were taught something positive about a Black person, a white savior was always involved. Black people were helped during slavery by the white abolitionists. Black people were freed from slavery because of the white savior Abraham Lincoln.

I remember repeatedly seeing images of Henry "Box" Brown throughout my childhood schooling. Brown had escaped slavery in the South with the help of white abolitionists in the North by being mailed in a box to Philadelphia, which was in a free state. There is a famous illustration of Brown being assisted out of his box, surrounded by white abolitionists.

I was also taught that Dr. Martin Luther King Jr. and other 60s Black activists were able to get the Civil Rights laws passed because of the kindness of white saviors like President Lyndon B. Johnson, who signed the bills into law.

Now, this same school, which minimized the accomplishments of almost every Black historical figure, had me sitting up here praying over a white football coach. This rubbed me the wrong way for a long time. It was only after I became an adult that I would gain clarity and understanding about why I had felt confused.

In the work of the legendary psychiatrist Dr. Frances Cress Welsing, I read her theories about sports and how they relate to the system of white supremacy. She described how white supremacy would also subconsciously manifest itself through symbols, objects, and activities. Since the basis of white supremacy is white genetic survival, certain symbolism in sports would reflect that fact. For example, she explained how on an abstract level, sports games involving large brown balls, such as football and basketball, represented Black male sexual organs. And the objective of these games is to prevent the brown balls from going into the white field goal or white nets, which represent the white female sexual orifice.

Dr. Welsing also explained how games involving small white balls, such as baseball and golf, use large phallic equipment like bats and clubs to hit the white balls away from the body. She explained how this is a subconscious act of self-deprecation when observed in the abstract. The white supremacist male subconscious rejects his own genitalia because of an innate feeling of inadequacy when compared to the power of Black male genitalia.

Dr. Welsing went on to explain that this is one of the reasons Black males were not permitted to play golf professionally for a long time. Tiger Woods was one of the few exceptions to break through. And notice how, over the years, the white media has criminalized him and portrayed him as a sexual predator because of his consensual sexual relationships with white women.

People who believe in white supremacy view sports differently than others. They look at sports as a metaphor for their genetic survival. This is why they often have a religious fanaticism about sports. Suspected white supremacist sports fans around the world have a long track record of open racial antagonism towards Black players in particular. At soccer games throughout Europe and in other white identified countries, racist sports fans are infamous for spewing racial slurs and directing racist chants towards Black soccer players.

In the United States, Black athletes have been historically subject to racial antagonism as well. The suspected white supremacists have learned to cope with Black athletes as long as the coaches are majority white, the quarterbacks – who controls the "brown balls" – are majority white, and the Black players don't get too uppity (like Colin Kaepernick) and start calling out systematic white supremacy.

When looking at things from the context of white supremacy, it is easy to understand why certain white football coaches like Coach Bear Bryant, who controlled mostly Black players, are held up as messianic type figures. And are, therefore, deserving of mass prayer vigils during the middle of the school day.

The entire global system of white supremacy runs like a religion. The author Neely Fuller has suggested that white supremacy is the most powerful religion ever known to man.

The Origin of The Religion of White Supremacy

Dr. Frances Cress Welsing stated that racism and white supremacy were one and the same. There are no other systematic forms of racism besides white supremacy. Dr. Welsing concluded that a global system of white supremacy/racism was created because of a collective fear of white genetic annihilation. White supremacists believe that the most serious threat to the genetic survival of the white race is miscegenation, or race mixing. Black people have become the main targets and victims of the unjust system of white supremacy, with the Black male being particularly targeted. White supremacists have acknowledged that Black men have the genetic power to potentially neutralize the white bloodline simply by engaging in sexual intercourse with white women and producing offspring. Black sexuality is thus seen in the system of white supremacy as a form of warfare. This is why so many homicides of Black people committed by whites are generally viewed as justified, no matter the circumstance.

Few people have theorized about the origin of systematic white supremacy. Most white scholars only acknowledge white supremacy in the context of extremist groups like the Aryan Nation and the Ku Klux Klan, but they generally remain in denial about systematic white supremacy because they often benefit from that unjust system.

Many Black scholars don't dig into the origins of white supremacy because they usually don't want to rock the boat among their academic circles. Many don't want to offend white people.

Some scholars trace the concept of racism to the caste system of ancient India, but that system was primarily based on class and status and it did not branch out to become a global phenomenon at the time, with Indians dominating large groups of people based on that system. Interestingly, many of the titles and symbols from the Indian caste system, like the Aryan designation and the Hindu symbol -now known as the swastika, were later adopted by the white supremacist Nazis.

From my studies, it appears that the global phenomenon of systematic white supremacy originated in Spain in the Middle Ages. After the fall of the Roman Empire around the year 476 AD, European society regressed into what's commonly referred to as the Dark Ages. Extensive warfare, economic collapse, and devastating disease were rampant across Europe.

In fact, around the year 541 AD, the Plague of Justinian, one of the first recorded mass pandemics, killed over half the population of Europe (Mordechai et al., 2019; Spyrou, Maria et al., 2016). In some cities, up to 5000 people were dying per day.

Many of the people dying off were the builders, the craftsmen, the soldiers, and other significant people needed to maintain a functioning society. Europe remained in a degenerate and weakened state for centuries. In the year 711 AD, a group of majority Black men from Africa called the Moors crossed into Spain (Fletcher 2006; Glick, 2005) and conquered the Iberian peninsula.

While the Moors occupied Spain, they brought with them advanced science, architecture, education, and medicines that resonated across Europe. Some of the medicines the Moors brought to Europe helped to eradicate some of the endemic diseases. The last outbreak of the Justinian Plague was eliminated in the year 750 AD after the Moors arrived in Europe (Alfani, 2017; Little & Walsh, 2007).

During the height of Moorish rule in Spain, Córdoba was the most modern city in Europe (Hillenbard, 1992; Nayler, 2017). The streets were well-paved, with raised sidewalks for pedestrians. The Moors also established seventeen great universities that were located in Almeria, Cordova, Granada, Juen, Malaga, Seville, and Toledo. Moorish rule brought with it significant advantages and progress.

But there was also a perceived disadvantage. Because the Moors dominated society at the time, they also had unlimited and unregulated sexual access to European women. These sexual unions between European women and the Black Moors produced dark offspring. In European societies where the Moors were most prevalent, such as Spain and parts of Italy, the Moors essentially created a fixed mulatto race. Even today, many Spanish and Southern Italians are phenotypically darker than other Europeans. This is due to the presence of the Moors.

At a certain point during the reign of the Moors in Spain, some Europeans realized that their ethnic bloodlines were slowly being wiped out. The Europeans then launched what is known historically as the *Reconquista*, or the Reconquest of Spain from Moorish rule. For 800 years the Moors ruled Spain, and the Europeans took advantage of in-fighting between various Moorish kingdoms throughout the Iberian peninsula to reestablish white rule. The Europeans slowly conquered each individual kingdom and pushed the Moors further south.

The Reconquista has always been framed as a Holy War between Christians and Muslims, but it was really war between white Europeans and Black Moors in an effort to save the European bloodline.

This is the birthplace of the white supremacist religions. In the year 1449, the Spanish Kingdom of Castile would be the first European society to implement blood purity statutes (Edwards, 1990; Martinez, 2008). This policy was called the *limpieza de sangre*, which means "cleanliness of blood", and it was used to enact discriminatory practices against people who had Moorish or Jewish blood.

This desire for Europeans to expunge this ethnic "other" group, and maintain the purity of their own ethnic bloodline, led to the creation of the first nation state in Europe (Graves, Joseph et al., 2003). Before Spain in the late 1400s, there were no coherent nations in Europe (Ruiz, 2014). The territories consisted of scattered decentralized kingdoms and villages.

The nation state of Spain was solidified when the kingdoms of Aragon and Castile consolidated their power and military to drive the remaining Moors from the city of Grenada. When the Spanish finally defeated the Moors in 1492, Spain also became the first European global empire. Victory was celebrated with ritualistic celebrations that carried racial undertones, like the running of the bulls. In this ritualistic celebration, the people of Spain dress in white outfits and chase a black bull around the streets. Dr. Frances Cress Welsing wrote that this symbolizes the white Europeans running the black Moors out of Spain.

There is another annual tradition in Spain called *Semana Santa*, or Holy Week. In this tradition, the white people of Spain celebrate the expulsion of the Moors by dressing in robes and pointed hats (Coyle, 1996; Metz, 1986), attire the white supremacist terrorist organization the Ku Klux Klan later adopted. The Klan too claims to be a Christian organization. Modern white supremacists are fully aware of the racial significance of the Reconquista of Spain.

Recently, a white supremacist named Brenton Tarrant went on a killing spree and massacred dozens of non-white Muslims at two mosques in New Zealand. Tarrant wrote a manifesto that stated his motivations. He wrote:

(I carried out the attacks) "to take revenge on the invaders for the hundreds of thousands of deaths caused by foreign invaders in European lands throughout history."

He continued: "To take revenge for the enslavement of millions of Europeans taken from their lands by the Islamic slavers."

The racial holy war that started in Europe against the Moors continues to this day. The term Moor was simply a descriptive term. Europeans in the Middle Ages referred to all Black people or very dark individuals as Moors. The etymology of the word Moor comes from the words black or dark (Adler 1974; Cozmo El, 2016). Eventually, the Europeans started to use the term Black and Moor interchangeably to describe people of African descent. In many instances, they combined the words and used the term Blackamoor to describe Black people. The Spanish word for black is *negro*, and in the mid-1500s the word negro was splintered and morphed into the pejorative term, "nigger" (Moore, 1992; Pryor, 2016).

In the collective psyche of the European colonizers, Black people had to be dehumanized so that the Europeans could justify the creation of a concept of white supremacy. When Spanish explorers started to venture outside of Europe, they realized they were on a planet surrounded by melanated people. They also realized that procreating with these people would produce non-white offspring. In order to survive genetically, they had to create a system of perpetual subjugation for the non-white people of the planet.

White supremacists will often try to promote the fallacy that this subjugation is based on traditional religious differences instead of racial domination. This leads non-white victims of racism to believe that if they simply convert to the religion of their white oppressors, they will somehow be safe from racial terrorism. Some of the most devout Christians are Black people, and white supremacists, including white Christians, have a long history of mistreating Black people. Most churches in America and around the world remain racially segregated.

Black Christians generally aren't accepted as a group among white Christians today, just like many of the Moriscos, descended from the Black Moors, we're not fully accepted in Spain. The Moriscos converted to Christianity in Spain but still were not accepted by the Spanish and were ultimately expelled from Spain (Jónsson, 2007). They were expelled based on race, because the religion of white supremacy trumps every other religion.

Rules of the Religion of White Supremacy

The people who have maintained systematic white supremacy over the last few centuries have been able to do so by abiding by written and unwritten rules and codes. When the system of white supremacy was initially being put into place, the white supremacists were very open about their motives and agenda.

Now, most people in the dominant society pick up these rules and codes through osmosis.

In the early part of the 20th Century, a series of books were released that did not beat around the bush in their promotion of white supremacy. *The Negro: A Menace To American Society* by Robert Wilson Shufeldt, and many others used pseudoscience and religion to justify the practice of anti-Black racism.

A book released in 1913 by an educator and white supremacist named Thomas P. Bailey, entitled *Race Orthodoxy In The South*, provided one of the most accurate summaries of the rules of white supremacy.

In one section of the book, Bailey gave a list of 15 aspects of the "Southern" creed, which was really the general white supremacist creed. Bailey stated that this creed was "practically the common opinion of the South."

The 15 points of this white supremacist creed are:

1. Blood will tell
2. The white race must dominate
3. The Teutonic people stand for race purity
4. The negro is inferior and will remain so
5. This is a white man's country
6. No social equality
7. No political equality
8. In matters of civil rights and legal adjustments give the white man as opposed to the colored man the

benefit of the doubt; and under no circumstances interfere with the prestige of the white race

9. In educational policy, let the negro have the crumbs that fall from the white man's table
10. Let there be such industrial education of the negro as will best fit him to serve the white man
11. Only Southerners understand the negro question
12. Let the South settle the negro question
13. The status of peasantry is all the negro may hope for, if the races are to live together in peace
14. Let the lowest white man count for more than the highest negro
15. The above statements indicate the leadings of Providence

Every rule in this white supremacist creed is practiced to the fullest extent today, in every area of activity. The only difference now is that these rules are never to be spoken publicly, and the existence of these rules are to be denied at all costs.

CHAPTER FOUR

Common Misconceptions About White Supremacy

When I was around 8 years old, my mother and I moved into a house on Fulton Avenue in an area of Birmingham called West End. I would live between this house and my grandmother's house in Leeds for the next decade. But I spent most of these years in West End. I loved West End. There was a small amusement park called Kiddieland on the Alabama State Fairgrounds that was walking distance from my house. I would go there almost every other day. Another thing I liked about West End was that it wasn't as slow paced as Leeds. This was a time when children were required to go outside and it was relatively safe for kids to run around outside and socialize. The only time around this period that I can remember there were safety concerns about children going outside was during the Atlanta Child Murders that were happening in the neighboring state of Georgia. But when the fear from that tragedy dissipated, things went back to normal. I made a lot of friends in the neighborhood and we would kick it outside everyday after school.

When we first moved to West End it was a racially mixed working class community. Over the next few years, more and more white families moved out of the area, and when they moved out, they took the tax bracket with them. Most of society's industries and resources are generationally locked in and racially secured by the dominant society. When white flight happens, it often leaves behind a Scorched Earth effect in the neighborhood or city.

In the 70s and 80s, when white families were fleeing en masse from newly integrated areas and taking the economic resources with them, many of these cities started to elect Black mayors and other Black elected officials into local office. As long as the governors of these states remained white (because the governor's office is in charge of allocating a state's resources), many people in the dominant society had no problem propping up Black local officials. This is probably why there have been only four Black governors in the entire history of the continental United States (David Paterson, Deval Patrick, P.B.S Pinchback, and Douglas Wilder). And two of those governors, P. B. S. Pinchback, who served as governor of Louisiana in 1872, and Douglas Wilder, who served in Virginia in 1990, could pass for white.

In 1979, the city of Birmingham elected its first Black mayor, Richard Arrington, who would remain in office for 20 years. Mayor Arrington was propped up as a mascot for racial equality in a city that was still raw with the scars of the civil rights struggle. This was the template for many urban areas around the country at the time. White-controlled think tanks would carefully vet a Black person and groom them as a political tool for the establishment.

Many of these Black elected officials are associated with an organization that fancies itself a Black secret society, The Boule. This organization has been around since the early 1900s and the general purpose of this fraternity is to cultivate those they consider to be the "talented tenth" of Black society. The term Boule means "advisor to the king", and this organization's criteria for talented tenth status is based on their social, political and educational proximity to white society.

The Boule is a secret to most of Black society, but the white establishment is very aware of them. The white establishment understands that many of the Boule members desire approval from white society. And the establishment knows how to exploit this to its advantage.

Boule members are often placed in political positions in cities with significant Black populations and they are rewarded with status and job security. And, in most cases, nothing is done to provide tangible resources to the Black population. This was the case with Richard Arrington, a Boule member, who was put into office in Birmingham.

I watched certain areas of Birmingham, and West End in particular, slowly degenerate from a neighborhood into a "hood" throughout the early 80s. Property values were slowly declining, and we started to see more and more abandoned homes in the area.

There was an increase in petty crime in the area as well. I remember our home on Fulton Avenue being broken into several times when I was in school and my mother was at work. We started to see a few drug addicts trickle in and wander around the area. The same scenario played out in cities all over the country.

The general misconception about this phenomenon of urban decay was that it was due to Black incompetence. White supremacist society would point to these urban areas and their general consensus was "this is what happens when Black people are in control." Consequently, Black people would internalize this same consensus. As a child, I never internalized, nor did I accept, the self-deprecating narrative that melanated skin somehow caused a sector of society to automatically fail.

I knew instinctively that other forces were at play. Eventually I would come to understand how white supremacists systematically orchestrate every facet of this racially based deprivation of resources.

White supremacy is warfare and all warfare is based on deception. White supremacists go to great lengths to constantly deceive non-white people on the planet, particularly Black people. This causes the victims of this deception to develop several misconceptions about white supremacy.

Here are five of the most common myths and misconceptions Black people have about white supremacy. Understanding these misconceptions and countering them can bring victims of racism many steps forward in their efforts to replace the system of white supremacy with a system of justice.

Myth #1. All White Supremacists Are Aggressive and Hostile

Hands down this is one of the biggest misconceptions Black people have about white supremacy. Many Black people think that if a suspected white supremacist is courteous or even nice to them, that person could not possibly be an anti-Black racist. Nothing could be further from the truth.

White supremacists have always played the good cop/bad cop role around Black people. Some white people will openly argue against certain white extremist groups. We take notice of this routine and assume that they are at odds with each other. But in reality, they are on-code with one another. Usually the objective is to maintain systematic racial dominance by any means.

Black people are taught that a white supremacist is a hostile person, who runs around in a Klan robe burning down Black churches while yelling nigger. If this was the normal manifestation of white supremacy, it would not have the same long-lasting effectiveness. Such behavior would keep Black people on constant alert. If Black people are overtly alerted to white supremacist tactics, they would consciously and collectively start to develop effective defenses against these tactics.

The most effective white supremacists are the ones who approach Black people in a polite, covert manner, often causing Black people to lower their defenses. Black people are more effectively undermined by the white supremacists when this approach is utilized.

Myth #2. Black People's Actions Cause White Supremacist Backlash

Many Black people spend a lot of time trying to regulate their behavior in order to appease white society. We are often taught from a young age that, in order to survive and make a living, we must act in a manner that is non-offensive to white society.

We are told that white society must target Black people for systematic punishment because Black people have an inherently flawed culture. Even if a Black person does not display these allegedly inherent flawed cultural characteristics, the punishment of Black people is still justified. White supremacists reason that one bad apple spoils the whole group.

In a futile effort to curtail this systematic and racially targeted punishment, Black society often engages in a rigid form of respectability politics. We try to live up to an impossible standard of good cultural behavior. If anyone Black doesn't live up to these cultural standards, we are programmed to believe it is our melanated skin that is the problem. Therefore, we must believe that we deserve the punishment white society doles out to us.

Black people collectively internalize the criminalization stigma that white supremacist society projects onto them. Black people are the only group that is made to take collective responsibility for criminal elements in our society. White supremacists go out of their way to embed propaganda that Black people are inherently criminal and violent.

The reality is that almost all "Black crime" in the United States is isolated to economically depressed enclaves. Patterns of crime and violence are almost nonexistent in the middle class and well-to-do sectors of Black society. Other racial and ethnic groups have entire large-scale organized criminal enterprises that eclipse the petty criminality that occurs in Black society. In fact, other so-called "model minority" groups are often the ones who facilitate the import of illegal substances, weapons and other entities into Black populated areas. Many of the drugs and guns in Black society are brought in by Hispanic and Asian organized crime groups.

There are violent organized Asian gangs like the Triads, the Yakuza and others, and countless Hispanic drug cartels all over Latin America, whose criminal operations spill over into the United States.

The difference between these criminals from immigrant backgrounds and Black people, is that law enforcement often gives a green light to the illegal activities of these other non-

Black groups. The dominant society understands the importance of having these immigrant groups propped up as a buffer class over Black society. And one of the selling points to get these buffer classes on board is to have the legal system act more leniently towards enforcing the law against their criminal element.

Aside from the criminality and violence of non-Black buffer groups, it is white supremacists who are the most violent group in recorded history. They have killed each other in Europe going back thousands of years. Terms that we use today that are synonymous with violence and savagery, like "vandal" and "barbarian", were the names of European tribes (Goffart, 2020; Merrills & Miles, 2009).

Throughout history, white supremacists killed and enslaved millions of Africans. They killed millions of people in India and Australia. They committed complete genocide against the people of Tasmania (Lawson, 2014; Madley, 2009). They killed scores of Polynesian people throughout the Pacific Ocean region (Oliver, 1989; Taylor, 2020). In the Americas they wiped out millions of Native Americans. In the early 20th century, they started killing other Europeans. Millions of people died in the Ukraine in 1932 and 1933 during the Famine-Genocide. And white supremacists in Nazi Germany killed millions of other Europeans who they felt were not white enough.

Violent crimes based on racially targeted economic deprivation, in which only a small sector of Black society is engaged, cannot compare to the long history of white supremacist violence.

Myth #3. Racism/White Supremacy is Based on Ignorance

The narrative that people in the dominant society practice racism because they "don't know any better" is a common misconception that Black people love to promote. Many Black people do not want to accept the fact that we are in a global system of white supremacist domination where anti-Black racists are 100% conscious of the system they are maintaining.

By going along with the fallacy that white supremacists are not aware of their participation in this racially terroristic system, many Black people can wiggle their way out of confronting, fighting and rejecting this system. This is because many Black people do not want to admit that the thought of challenging the system of white supremacy scares them.

Instead, many Black people play this game of trying to educate suspected white supremacists on the negative effects of racism. Black people try to use their expertise in being victims of white supremacy as "educational credentials" to teach white people about racism.

Black people cannot teach suspected white supremacists about racism for two main reasons:

1. White supremacists created the system of racism/white supremacy. This includes all the racial categories, racial slave codes, Jim Crow laws, eugenics programs, the racially based prison industrial complex, and the racially biased legal and educational systems.

There is nothing a Black person can teach the masters and architects of systematic racism about white supremacy.

2. White people are already expected to understand the system, or they will likely get in trouble with other suspected white supremacists if they do not follow the codes of white supremacy. Author Neely Fuller has stated that by the age of 15, the average white person has a general understanding of white supremacy/racism. In many cases, it's earlier. For example, if a white person appears to be too accommodating to a Black person or Black people, they risk being labeled a nigger lover.

Young people like to rebel against societal norms. When white youths are being taught the codes and rules of white supremacy, many instinctively recognize how wrong and unjust the rules are. So they will often rebel.

The most common form of rebellion is to emulate the underbelly of Black culture. They will listen to the most derogatory forms of rap music and adopt a "hood" vernacular. But, in most cases, they do not rebel to the point where they might lose their white privileges. White youths are given leeway to temporarily rebel to a certain extent because, as they get older and the acquisition of resources becomes more competitive, they will quickly use the white privileges that come along with systematic white supremacy in order to get a leg up.

White people are expected to conduct themselves in a certain way in their interactions with Black people. This is especially true when that interaction has a broader effect on society at large. A white person will often choose to maintain systematic white supremacy- which is the basis for the white privileges from which they benefit- over equal justice for non-white people.

A globally sophisticated system like white supremacy cannot be maintained for as long as it has been maintained without the participants and beneficiaries consciously understanding how racism is required to perpetuate the system.

White society is fully aware of the systematic mistreatment of Black people. They are also aware of the unearned gains, benefits and privileges that come with the subjugation of Black people. Nonetheless, it is more convenient for them to continue to receive those privileges while feigning naïveté to racial injustice.

Myth #4. White Supremacists Are Patriotic

White supremacists will often try to hide their racist views behind a veil of false patriotism. This con game was on full display during the kneeling controversy involving NFL player Colin Kaepernick. Kaepernick decided to protest the epidemic of racial killings of Black citizens by white police officers. He protested by kneeling during the National Anthem at NFL games. Many suspected white supremacists around the country, who were perfectly fine with the unjust, state sanctioned killings of Black citizens, tried to hide their complicity behind fake patriotism, claiming that Kaepernick was disrespecting the American flag.

Many white supremacist militia groups also try to shield their racist ideologies by giving their organizations patriotic names. Oftentimes they do so to justify stockpiling weapons under the 2nd Amendment. White supremacists are aware that part of their power comes from their priority access to a cache of weapons, and a general immunity from prosecution. When Black people stockpile weapons, they risk being put on some type of government watch list or even worse.

But white supremacists are allowed to stockpile an arsenal of weapons basically unchecked, until one of them commits a mass shooting. Many of the pretend patriots who are always waving the American flag and talking about the constitution are the same people plotting to take down the American government. White supremacist terrorist Timothy McVeigh was part of the Patriot movement (Durham, 1996) before he attacked the federal building in Oklahoma City, killing and injuring nearly a thousand people. McVeigh viewed his actions as an attack on the American government.

Modern white extremist groups, such as The Base, have also plotted to take down and destroy the American government (Byman, 2021; Hoffman, 1995). Many of their members were recruited from patriot movements. On January 6th, 2021, large groups of suspected white supremacist "patriots" violently stormed the United States Capitol building in Washington D.C. in a failed attempt to overthrow the U.S. Government.

White supremacists don't really believe in *geographical* governments because white supremacy is its own government. This is why they can set up a white supremacist regime anywhere on the planet with the exception of North Sentinel Island. This island in the middle of the Indian Ocean is inhabited by a tribe of Black natives who have lived there for over 60,000 years. They will kill any outsider visiting the island onsight. So the white supremacists do not attempt to go to that particular island because the people there have let it be known that they will not be colonized, and they are willing to kill or be killed in order to protect their environment and culture. And if the white supremacists have to kill all the inhabitants of a particular region, without receiving some material gain, that defeats the purpose of white supremacy. They need non-white people around to be supreme over.

The white supremacists are only patriotic to the religion of white supremacy. They will throw out the American flag in a heartbeat the moment they feel the American government is not upholding the system of white supremacy to their standards. It was white supremacists who formed the Confederacy in the Southern United States and went to war against the American flag. Self-admitted white supremacists, the Confederate leaders repeatedly gave speeches touting their white supremacist ideology.

The creator of the Confederate Flag, William Tappan Thompson, said his flag was "the white man's flag (Cunningham, 2017)." Thompson also wrote a series of essays, going on about how superior the white race was. One of his more famous quotes:

"As a people, we are fighting to maintain the heaven ordained supremacy of the white man over the inferior or colored race: a white flag would thus be emblematical of our cause" (Coope, 2018; Lowery, 2016).

A few years ago, I went to a Floyd Mayweather fight in Las Vegas where he fought the Irish boxer Connor McGregor. This fight had all the racial undertones of every other professional fight that featured a Black boxer and a great white hope opponent.

Mayweather, the Foundational Black American fighter, was representing the American flag. McGregor was representing the flag of Ireland. Throughout Las Vegas on the day of the fight, there were thousands of white Americans running around Las Vegas with Irish flags. I was one of the very few people who had an American flag wrapped around my shoulders.

Almost every place in Vegas that had Irish flags for sale was sold out. But American flags were fully available everywhere because people weren't buying them.

Whenever a Black American fighter competes with a foreign fighter from a non-Black country, white American fight fans will usually side with the foreigner. White audiences will usually give foreign Hispanic or Asian fighters honorary white status if they are competing against a Black American fighter (many white boxing fans also sided with another famous opponent of Floyd Mayweather, the Asian boxer Manny Pacquiao). This is because their allegiance is to white supremacy and not a particular country or region. Patriotism goes out the window when it comes to bestowing on or sharing that patriotism with Black people.

Myth #5. Racism Goes Both Ways

White supremacists usually try to distract from their own racism by trying to project their racist ideologies onto others. They try to use terms like "reverse racism" to create the illusion that there is some type of comparative racism that non-white people practice against them.

The white supremacists will often try to push a false narrative about the existence of "Black racism", but they are fully aware that systematic Black racism doesn't exist. They will even try to go so far as to use terms like "Black supremacist." But logic cancels out that narrative because the word "supreme" means highest in rank or authority. Supreme means the end all be all. And by definition there cannot be two supremes.

White supremacy/racism is an entire global system that negatively impacts the lives of non-white people in all areas of activity. Black racism basically amounts to name-calling. A Black person might use a racial insult to address a white person or another race, but that is the extent of Black racism. There is a *system* in place that will quickly and severely punish Black people for causing any type of physical harm to a white person.

Many in white society will try to compare the systematic anti-Black subjugation that dominates the educational system, medical field, judicial system, employment system, and so on, to a Black person hurling an insult like "honky" or "cracker" towards a white person. In the United States, the buffer class groups are now being used to push the "Blacks are the real racists" narrative. People in Asian American society are allowed to spew anti-Black epithets and even physically abuse Black women customers who patronize Asian owned establishments. Asians are rarely prosecuted for these common anti-Black crimes. But in certain states, Black people are severely punished with federal hate crime charges simply for saying something that might be perceived as insulting to an Asian person.

There is no such thing as systematic Black racism, and the white supremacists are fully aware of this. There is only one form of systemic racism: white supremacy.

CHAPTER FIVE

Race and Relationships

My first bestselling book, called *The Art of Mackin*, was released in 2000. It was a new urban twist on the relationship books that dominated the market at the time. Initially the book was marketed towards Black and urban demographics. Because of its popularity and grassroots success, the book crossed over to dominant society.

I would eventually receive many emails from readers asking for dating advice or posing general questions about the book. I noticed that many questions I received were various racial inquiries, particularly from white readers. The most common question was if the information contained in the book would work for white guys. I initially thought that these questions were odd because I thought, why wouldn't this information work for white people or other races? But, as I eventually grew to better understand the white supremacist mindset, things would become clearer.

This issue that some of these people were having was not a cultural inability to understand and apply the information from my book. The real issue was coming to terms with the fact that they were getting constructive advice and information about a topic as sensitive as relationships from a Black man. Some people from dominant society have apprehensions about Black men who are authority figures on particular issues. This is especially true for relationships and dating.

For years in the United States, laws were in place that regulated and criminalized Black men's access to certain relationships. Different types of miscegenation laws, as well as the concept of marriage licenses, were introduced in the 1920s as a way to prevent white and Black people from marrying (Cruz & Berson, 2001; Pascoe, 2009).

White supremacists are hyper-sensitive about issues related to dating and relationships because dating leads to intimacy, and intimacy ultimately leads to procreation. White supremacists are very concerned about anything that has to do with human procreation because of their fear of genetic annihilation. According to Neely Fuller, sex is the second most power motivating force after white supremacy.

Black audiences have always been trendsetters. Whenever something becomes popular among Black audiences (or as market researchers call it, the "urban demographic"), white corporations and media will immediately jump on that trend and find ways to market it to the dominant society. In many cases, when a trend or entity crosses over after Black audiences have given it street credibility, it will be coopted by the dominant society altogether. This has happened with several music genres such as rock & roll, jazz, and so on.

A few years after *The Art of Mackin'* was released, it proved that there was a viable market for men seeking relationship advice from a non-clinical perspective, and the corporate media immediately took notice. I got two separate book deals from major book publishers to put out my follow up books, *Play Or Be Played* and *The Mack Within*.

After my book *The Art of Mackin'* proved to be a commercial success, the modern pick-up artist, or PUA, movement emerged. Most of these PUAs were white guys who started writing books that gave similar dating advice. Later, many of these white dating experts and PUAs became affiliated with the alt-right white supremacist movement.

The combination of race and relationships is a central theme in the mind of the white supremacist. Because of their fear of genetic annihilation, they have to always be aware of societal trends about interactions between Blacks and whites. They make sure that Black interactions with white society is generally from a subordinate position. When Black people are in a powerless, subordinate position, white supremacists can better dictate and control the lives of their Black victims.

When Black people are in a sexual or other type of intimate relationship with people classified as white, Black people still remain in a powerless, subordinate position. This dynamic confuses many Black people because they are often under the illusion that a white person engaged in intimate relations with a Black person could not possibly be a racist. These people need to remember that it was a standard practice for white slave owners to sexually interact with their Black female and male slaves. After these sexual assaults and rapes were over for the night, the white slave owners made sure that their victims were back in the cotton fields working the next morning.

Tragic Arrangements

To add to the philosophy of Neely Fuller, Black people don't really have relationships with white society – we often have tacky tragic arrangements. Because Black people are in a systematic subordinate position to white society globally, intimate relationships with white people reflect those dynamics.

The physical act of consensual sexual intercourse often gives the illusion of social equality. On the surface, the two naked people engaged in the sexual encounter are temporarily equal in a physical sense. This is why many Black people try to over-perform sexually when they are intimate with white people.

When the sex act is completed between a Black person and a white person, the white person is now in a position to practice racial dominance over the Black person. The white person has the option to chose whether or not they will invoke their white privilege. Just the fact that Black people are in a tragic position where they have to hope that a white person doesn't invoke their right to practice white supremacy proves this is a dangerous existence.

When a white person gets out of a bed with a Black person, that white person has an entire system of white supremacy that will generally protect them from any type of harm or attempted injustice from the Black person.

In many cases, when Black women get involved in intimate situations with white men and the woman ends up missing, harmed or dead, the white man is oftentimes untouched by the law. In cases where white women have consensual sexual relations with Black men, and they turn around and claim that they were raped, white society usually gives them the benefit of the doubt as well as protection.

Many relationships between Black people and non-Black people are genuinely based in love and mutual admiration. But too often Black men and women engage in intimate relationships with whites that are exploitive. There are generally three sexually stereotypical categories into which white supremacist society places Black men. Black women are put into three additional categories. For Black women, these categories are:

1. The Negro Bed Wench

During antebellum slavery, white supremacist slave owners made it part of their culture to regularly rape Black women. Many Black women vigorously resisted this sexual exploitation. Runaway slave notices often revealed that a high number of the slaves who ran away from their slave owners were female house slaves, likely due to the repeated sexual assaults that enslaved women suffered. These brave women were willing to risk death to escape from the sexually deranged slave owners before they would remain under that type of subjugation.

Unfortunately many of the victims of this culture of white supremacist sexual abuse would ultimately be broken down psychologically. These victims eventually became actively complicit in thwarting any uprising or rebellion that might upset the order of systematic subjugation under the plantation system.

Many Bed Wenches imagined themselves to be honorary white supremacists as a way to cope with the tragic arrangement of being sexually fetishized and exploited. Many of these women felt they had to go along to get along.

Being forced into being a Bed Wench, and having a Negro Bed Wench mentality are two different things. Many enslaved women who were physically forced into sexual exploitive captivity by white supremacists were not *mentally* complicit. This is why so many of these women fled their owners. A person with a Bed Wench *mentality* is, however, an enemy of Black society. The character Sheba from the movie Django accurately represents the Negro Bed Wench mentality. In the film, the Sheba character was allowed by her white slave master to live a life of relative leisure. The slave owner Calvin Candy, played by Leonardo DiCaprio, chose Sheba to be his favored bed wench, and she was allowed to wear finer clothing, eat better food, and drink fine wines. Her illusionary status as a sexual equal of her slave master caused her to see other Black characters in the film through the eyes of the white supremacists.

Several scenes in the movie depicted the Sheba character looking at her fellow slave Django with disdain. She didn't even want to sit next to Django because she felt that he was beneath her.

This type of delusional Negro Bed Wench mentality plays itself out in current real-life scenarios. This mentality is mostly prevalent among non-Foundational Black American females. Many non-FBA females come from African or Caribbean countries where there are segments within those cultures that harbor anti-Black American sentiments. Most Black people from these countries generally have a courteous disposition towards Foundational Black Americans. The people who are allowed to immigrate from those countries to the U.S., however, are usually the ones who have proven to the white supremacists that they will go above and beyond to distance themselves from Foundational Black Americans and do the bidding of the white supremacists.

Another thing about certain African and Caribbean cultures, is that many of them are taught to view white people, particularly white men, in a different way than Foundational Black Americans view them. White supremacists control all nations around the globe, whether directly or indirectly. Foundational Black Americans are generally aware of this because we live in a nation where there is a white majority. We see the negative impact of white supremacist society on Black society on a daily basis.

In many African and Caribbean nations, the majority population is Black, so any form of social dilapidation has a Black face. When a white person shows up, they usually have some sort of minor tangible, such as food and clothing, they offer to the Black native peoples.

Even though suspected white supremacists show up in certain parts of these nations acting as missionaries and good samaritans, they are usually in cahoots with the white supremacists who contributed to the degeneration of these nations in the first place.

Many people in these Black populations do not comprehend the indirect impact that white supremacists have on their society. Whenever a white person shows up acting somewhat cordial, many Black inhabitants see them as a savior figure.

When they are allowed to immigrate to the United States, or if they are anchored here by one or both of their immigrant parents, they often bring that white savior mentality with them. Because they do not feel like they have an ancestral camaraderie with Foundational Black Americans, it's very easy for them to side with white supremacists against us.

Women will generally take on the same mindset as the men they date. When certain non-white women date suspected white supremacist males, they often take on the ideologies of these men. When someone with the Negro Bed Wench mentality gets some form of validation from white supremacists, these women will often go out of their way to conduct themselves as mascots for white supremacy.

The tragic irony of many women with the Negro Bed Wench mentality is that they are often disposed of, both figuratively and literally, by their suspected white supremacist men. There are several instances from around the world where Black women are, on average, found missing or killed by their white boyfriends or husbands at high rates. Even more frequently, Black women are racially degraded by their white male significant others or their white family members.

Women with the Negro Bed Wench mentality are frequently tossed aside or disposed of by the white males with whom they are in arrangements, especially when they get older, because white society does not want its generational wealth passed down to Black people. It is very rare to see an older interracial white man/Black woman couple.

White men will keep these women around because they enjoy having plantation sex. But after the novelty of the exotic sexual escapades wears off, white males will often stay within the white supremacist code and treat the Black women they are involved with as subordinates.

2. The Jezebel Breeder

During antebellum slavery, many Black women were forced to be designated breeders by white supremacist slaveowners. In order to justify this inhumane treatment, white supremacists came up with the myth of the primitive and promiscuous Black woman.

This myth ran counter to the mid-19th-century ideal of the sophisticated Victorian white lady. White supremacists used the image of semi-nude women in Africa, who would do tribal dances that were reinterpreted as sexually lewd, to further justify their sexual abuse of Black women.

Because the Black woman was considered to be sexually undisciplined by nature, at least according to the rationale of the white supremacists, technically she could not be "raped" whenever white men took sexual liberties with her.

This twisted rationale was also used to justify breeding Black women on slave plantations for profit. The Jezebel Breeder stereotype was refined throughout the decades, and it continues today. The welfare queen narrative created in the 1970s and attributed to Black women was a continuation of the Jezebel Breeder image.

The narrative that sexually undisciplined Black women were having sexual relations with multiple men in order to have children that could then be used to game the welfare system was created and spread by white supremacists. In their minds, the idea that these Jezebel Breeders were using their inherently whorish disposition to gain unearned benefits, gave white supremacists the justification they needed to punish them, and by extension, punish Black society as a whole.

The dichotomy of the Jezebel Breeder stereotype is that it is both despised and encouraged by white supremacists. During antebellum slavery, the benefit of this forced arrangement came from the children this diabolical breeding process produced. Black children who were born from forced breeding were sold for a profit or forced to provide the free labor that benefitted white supremacists.

A modern, refined version of this phenomenon is the school to prison pipeline. In the late 1960s the Black family was systematically attacked through a number of social policies. Many Black women were incentivized to live in single parent households. Simultaneously, Black men were targeted with brutal state-sanctioned terrorism by race soldiers working in law enforcement.

This era was capped off with newly desegregated schools that were still run by the white supremacist system that mandated the previously segregated schools. These newly desegregated schools were consequently designed to covertly undermine the full development of Black children.

With all of these well orchestrated factors in place, white supremacists knew fully what the general outcome would be. Many Black children who came from some of these strategically broken homes, and placed in school systems that deliberately miseducated them, ultimately would be prime targets for the prison industrial complex.

And just as children were bred into the for-profit plantation system during antebellum slavery, children now are bred into the for-profit prison industrial system. White supremacists justify this evil system by blaming the victims. According to their narrative, the Jezebel Breeder is inherently flawed and transfers her dysfunctions to her children. This causes built-in criminality in these children that requires racial targeting by law enforcement to control these inherently flawed progeny of the Jezebel.

As ridiculous and false as this narrative is, the dominant society uses their "I'm white and I say so" rule to enforce it.

Women who are considered to be Jezebel Breeders by white society are generally relegated to impoverished neighborhoods. In certain areas it is common for lower class white men (and particularly white Hispanic males in coastal cities) to have sexual contact with these women by "slumming" with them.

Many biracial children from areas that are considered the "hood" are often the children of these lower class white men and the Jezebel Breeder.

3. The Exotic Oddity

The Hottentot Venus was the stage name given to a 19th century African woman named Sara Baartman. Baartman, who had an unusually large buttocks, was taken to Europe and exhibited as a freak show attraction.

European society fetishized Baartman's body and consequently she was exploited sexually by white men in Europe. Baartman was viewed with both sexual curiosity and disgust by European society. Europeans saw her as a grotesque, sexualized savage in comparison to the seemingly reserved image of European white women at the time, which helped reinforce the ideology of Black inferiority.

This image of the Exotic Oddity, contrast to white women as the standard norm, is still promoted today. The white media will often promote Black women who are morbidly obese in a sexual manner and place them next to slender or modelesque white women as an elaborate inside joke among white supremacists. For example, there have been instances where white supremacist high school students have elected an overweight Black girl as homecoming queen as a joke.

The Black actress Gabby Sidibe, who was extremely obese when she first appeared on the scene in Hollywood, was often placed on the cover of glamour magazines juxtaposed to slender white models and actresses. This was usually done as a back-handed compliment by white society. The white media tried to present this as a "body positivity" narrative, but in reality it was an inside joke among suspected white supremacists.

In the late 2000s, many Black people were calling on Hollywood to show more diversity. On social media there were discussions about the omission of Black faces in mainstream productions and in the modeling industry.

The response from the Hollywood system was to pacify complaints from Black people while simultaneously maintaining the image of white supremacy. Media and fashion magazines were saturated with images of Gabby Sidibe, portraying her as an Exotic Oddity in contrast to slim white actresses and models. This was meant to be a representation of Black culture.

The white media recently elevated an overweight Black female entertainer named Lizzo, who they also parade around like an Exotic Oddity. On one of her album covers they have her posed completely nude, and she is often featured in the media doing overtly sexual twerk dances.

Much like Gabby Sidibe, the white media tries to portray their exploitive coverage of Lizzo as an "embrace who you are and be comfortable" narrative. But overtly sexual images of Black women, who are considered physical oddities because of their size, are used to justify racially motivated punishments. The consensus among white supremacists is that if a person or group of people are inherently misshapen or overweight, it is a result of their laziness and undisciplined behavior. Therefore, they are not worthy of respect or equal treatment.

The 3 sexual categories into which Black men are generally placed by the dominant society are:

1. The Negro Bed Buck

During slavery, Black men were sexually exploited and reduced to being Negro Bed Bucks. Similar to the women forced into becoming Negro Bed Wenches for white supremacist slave owners, many Black men were forced into providing sexual gratification for both male and female slave owners.

Black men who have the Negro Bed Buck mentality today are generally men who hold white women in high esteem. White supremacist society still possesses direct and indirect ways to control sexual unions between Black men and white women. Nonetheless, they are typically fine with Black men who have the Negro Bed Buck mentality. They understand that the Bed Buck views white women as status symbols. The Bed Buck feels that his own self-worth as a Black man is so flawed within a system of white supremacy, that being able to achieve any semblance of companionship or affection with white women is the only way to correct this flaw.

White supremacists understand that a Black man with this type of mindset will not challenge or rebel against the very thing he worships. It's impossible to both praise and worship whiteness and seriously challenge systematic white supremacy.

The dichotomy is that white supremacists will dangle the carrot of sexual access to white women over the heads of Black men, yet whenever they feel like it they will also punish Black men for acting on that sexual access.

2. The Mandingo Fling

Many white women have experimental sexual relationships with Black men. Many white women grow up hearing rumors and Mandingo stereotypes about the sexual prowess of Black males, causing these white women to want to engage in a Mandingo Fling.

Some white women like to have one-off sexual experiments with Black men, while some go through a phase where they exclusively have sexual relations with Black men. Often, this is an act of rebellion. White women are told from early childhood not to date or marry Black men. White supremacist men have always had a homoerotic fixation with Black men's genitals and sexuality. This collective cultural insecurity actually creates a greater desire for white women to experiment with the forbidden negro. Many white women engage in Mandingo Flings during their college years or in their late teens or early 20s. Around this time, many white women who live in small, racially segregated Midwestern towns move to larger, more populated areas for college or careers. Once they get away from the scrutiny that comes with living in areas where everyone generally knows each other, they can engage in Mandingo Flings without stigma.

Systematic white supremacy is a form of socialism that guarantees people classified as white basic privileges, perks and protections. When these white women who have Mandingo Flings get a little older, they become more dependent on the racial perks and safety nets that come with the white supremacist socialist system.

Younger white women, especially those who are fairly attractive, often have everything given to them on a silver platter just by virtue of their youth. A popular phrase in White American culture during the Jim Crow era was "free, white and 21", which exemplified this privileged status. However, when these white women's beauty starts to fade, they have to compete with younger women and all those goodies start to dry up. Many begin to accept the white supremacist code.

Some of them go out of their way to hide their "swirling" past so they will not be tagged by white society with the nigger lover label. These women who have Mandingo Flings when they are young will often become actively racist as they get older in order to help maintain the system of white supremacy. The system provides them with basic necessities and privileges.

It is one reason why older white women are often among the most hardcore anti-Black racists. Several viral videos have circulated online of white women calling the police on innocent Black people and making false reports against them. Most of the white women in these videos are middle aged or older. These older white women become fierce defenders and foot soldiers for systematic white supremacy because without an unfair system of racial welfare and privileges to keep them afloat, many of these white women would be destitute.

Another way suspected white supremacist women try to get a pass from white society for having a Mandingo Fling is to use the Othello Excuse.

In the classic play, *Othello*, Shakespeare's central character Othello is a Black Moorish general married to a white woman named Desdemona. Desdemona's father Brabantio opposes the marriage and suggests that the only reason she could have possibly married the Black general is because he drugged her.

Narratives of white women being drugged by Black men in order to be sexually involved with them remains common today. The Bill Cosby situation, in which he was falsely accused of drugging several white women, is a modern version of the Othello Excuse.

Many of the Cosby's white accusers (and a few token non-white accusers, who come from white identifying, immigrant backgrounds, with cultures of contempt for Foundational

Black Americans) were proven to have lied about the drugging accusations. But white supremacist society got on code and used the "I'm white and I say so rule" to criminalize and convict Cosby of a sexual crime despite the fact that there was zero evidence. (White supremacists even claimed he confessed when transcripts from a previous deposition clearly proved Cosby denied giving women drugs against their knowledge for sexual purposes). Cosby eventually had the bogus conviction against him overturned after Pennsylvania's highest court determined that he was wrongly prosecuted.

Many Black men who fall into the Mandingo Fling category with white women are often confused by the racial politics of these relationships. They believe that white women who have sexual relations with them could not possibly have racist tendencies. Nothing can be further from the truth.

When many Black people have sexual relations with white people, they often come out of the situation confused or self-deceived. After an interracial sexual encounter they think they have somehow transcended racism or gained equal social status with white society. These Black people fail to recognize that white people can enjoy sexual pleasure from the victims of white supremacy, while also enjoying the privileges and benefits that come from the system of white supremacy.

3. The Eunuch

When African nations were initially invaded and conquered by outside forces, the conquerors, Arab invaders in particular, would often castrate young Black males and have them work as servants (King, 2011).

These Black men who were castrated and turned into eunuchs were often made to watch over the harems of women belonging to their male conquers. Black eunuchs were free to be around the women because they were no longer deemed to be a sexual threat.

Eunuchs were also dressed elaborately in flamboyant costumes by their conquerors, who paraded them around like prized and neutered pets. Fast forward to today, we see the dominant society is always more comfortable around buck broken, feminized Black men.

Not only is white society more comfortable with Black men who are social eunuchs, but it heavily promotes this non-gendered status to Black society. White supremacists understand that promoting and encouraging sexual confusion in Black society will lead to many beneficial outcomes for systematic white supremacy.

First, if Black people, particularly Black men, engage in non-sexual or same-sexual relations, this has the potential to reduce the Black population. This is because procreation cannot come from same-sex intercourse. Second, white supremacists understand that if they emasculate a Black male, that Black male will most likely not be a part of the warrior class of Black society that possesses the potential to rebel against systematic racism.

Most suspected white supremacist men feel more comfortable around buck broken Black men. Buck breaking is the term for a process during antebellum slavery where white slave owners and their white overseers sexually assaulted and raped Black men in front of the other slaves in order to break the spirit of the Black men and to show the other slaves that no Black man could save or protect them.

In the corporate world today, it is extremely rare to see a significant number of masculine, heterosexual Black men in equal positions with, or in equal proximity to, white men. Whenever I personally do business at white-owned corporate entities or media networks, there are always one or two Black men working there, and at least one of them will be non-heterosexual.

White men set up corporate institutions so that they can be the alpha males. Suspected white supremacist men are fully aware that they cannot compete with Black men on an equal level. They understand the need for systematic assistance to give them an extremely unfair advantage over Black men. This is why, for the most part, Black men base their identity on personal attributes. Because there are no systematic institutions solely controlled by Black men, traits centered around individual accomplishments like physical ability, personal talent, oratory skill, charisma, etc., become the priority.

Since white supremacist men generally cannot complete on an individual level, they prioritize certain institutional positions and occupations. These institutions become part of the white supremacist man's identity, and the last thing they will allow is a significant number of heterosexual Black men to trespass on that territory.

For the most part, white supremacists will allow Black men to take on a childlike disposition or they will allow Black men to become substitute Black *women*. When these Black men, who are perceived as eunuchs, circulate in corporate offices where there are white men and women, the white supremacist men are comforted to know that these men are not a sexual or genetic threat.

CHAPTER SIX

Racial Politics In The Workplace

I have never had a long-term square job in my life. I would get little temporary square gigs here and there in between street hustles or other endeavors that did not require me to have a boss looking over my shoulder.

Los Angeles in the early 1990s was very volatile terrain. On top of the high cost of living in Los Angeles County, the crack epidemic was still in full swing. Gang rivalries were at an all-time high. Hostile immigrant groups coming in from cultures with extreme anti-Black hatred were allowed to set up shop in Black neighborhoods. The LAPD was racially targeting Black people and funneling people in and out of jail on a regular basis.

The LAPD would do weekly "sweeps" where they would primarily target young Black males and arrest them for random, bogus infractions. Me, my friends, my associates, and many others would get caught up in this racial targeting. And we ended up being cycled in and out of jail at this time.

In between brief jail stints and street hustles, a lot of brothas in Los Angeles had to work temporary square jobs to get back on their feet. During the late 80s and early 90s, telemarketing jobs were everywhere in Los Angeles. Many street dudes and hustlers would work these jobs if they were fresh out of jail and in need of quick legit money. These places were also ideal because most didn't do any background checks or require a degree or even experience. And you could get paid relatively quickly.

A lot of my associates would work these telemarking gigs and some became managers. When I needed to make a few quick bucks, they would hook me up with one these jobs. Most of the telemarketing setups back then were barely legit themselves. These places were often owned by white collar criminals who would come up with questionable sales schemes in order to cash in. The locations would usually be in some type of boiler room or cheap rented office, and the employees usually consisted of struggling artists, hood dudes, and white drug addicts.

However, I learned early that even at the bottom of the social barrel, racial politics and racial hierarchy still existed. I was on one particular telemarketing job for a few months and every few weeks the white owners would hold contests among the telemarketers. They would give bonuses to the person who made the most sales for the week. I was fairly decent on the phones as far as sales, and I started getting good commissions, so I was waiting for another contest to come around.

One week, the owners announced they were going to give a $500 bonus to whichever employee made the most sales. I was going to step up my phone game and get that bonus because I really needed that extra paper at the time. At this particular office, there were around 15 telemarketers, called openers, in my department. Openers would make initial contact with potential clients and get them open to, or interested in buying whatever the company was selling. After we got them open to buying, we would collect their information, which was referred to as a "lead", and send it to a "closer", who was a more advanced and experienced sales person, in another section of the building, to close the deal.

I noticed that most of the "closers" were usually white guys. People in the closer position made more per hour and in commissions. In contrast, the openers were primarily Black men, Black women, white women, and one or two white men.

At this point, I'd been on this job for a few months. There was a new white man hired in the opener position named Allen. Allen had been there for a little over a week and he was a decent opener. He did pretty good on the phones and he generated a good amount of solid leads. Already we could tell that the owners were thinking about grooming him for a closer's position.

I wasn't planning to be at this job for the long term anyway, so I wasn't trippin' about that closer position. But I did want that $500 bonus. The week we were competing for that bonus, me and Allen were neck and neck in generating sales leads. A chalkboard in our department tracked our sales leads, so we could monitor each other's progress.

I started cranking up the calls and generating leads like crazy. And these were solid sales leads. Throughout the week, as we monitored the progress room, the chalkboard revealed I was in the lead and Allen was in second. When Friday rolled around, I was still leading on the chalkboard and when the contest was over at the end of the day, I was ready to get my bonus money and celebrate over the weekend.

The two company owners came out to announce the winner of the contest. I was completely thrown off guard when they announced Allen was the winner. I was standing there in disbelief and confusion, as was everyone else in the office. Naturally, we all wanted to know why Allen was the winner when I clearly had more sales leads on the board.

The owners basically used a version of the "I'm white and I say so" excuse by saying that even though I had more leads on the board, more of Allen's leads *closed* when they were sent to the closers. Naturally, this could not be verified and we just had to take the owners' word for it. At this point, I was extremely pissed off because I put in so much work during the week to generate those leads, yet I was not going to be properly rewarded for my work.

For the remainder of the day, the owners could feel that the energy in the office was uneasy. Everyone in our office area felt that the stunt the owners had pulled was a sleezy move. And the owners could see that my whole vibe was off, that I wasn't feeling the way things went down at all.

At the end of the shift the owners called me into their office to talk to me. I went into their office, sat down, and listened to them whitesplain' for five minutes, rambling on and on trying to explain why they rewarded Allen and not me, in a feeble attempt to pretend that it was something other than racial nepotism.

What I remember about the owners was that they were both named Dave. We called one "tall Dave" and the other "little Dave" because of their height difference. Tall Dave was a liberal hipster type. It was understood that he was more relatable and he would do daily motivational speeches to get everyone cranked up to hit the phones. Tall Dave had semi-long hair, and he would dress in a t-shirt and jeans around the office. Tall Dave did most of the "splainin'" during our private meeting.

Little Dave, on the other hand, was the total opposite. He wasn't quite a suit and tie type of guy, but he was more conservative and formal than Tall Dave. Little Dave was the numbers guy. He was the quintessential stern businessman.

During our private meeting, after Tall Dave did all his babbling, Little Dave chimed in and made me an offer. He said

"Tariq, I can understand if you are upset with the outcome of the contest. What we can do is determine the contest a tie. And we can split the $500 bonus between you and Allen, where you both get $250."

I told them to keep their money and quit the job. One reason I quit is because I refuse to play second fiddle to somebody I have outperformed. I have always had a competitive mentality where I refused to accept a position or situation that was less than I deserved. Even as a kid, I remember participating in dance contests around Birmingham. One particular contest, I knew I put in an excellent performance. Yet I ended up winning second place. I threw the 2nd place trophy away after they gave it to me. In my mind, accepting a second place trophy was equal to being complicit with injustice.

In the office with the two Daves, I knew that I could not be complicit in racially based policies that were clearly unjust. To accept this type of environment required that I think less of myself.

At the time I was still learning to live by a lot of rigid street codes. One thing I valued then, as I do now, is dignity. Compromising my dignity for any amount of money, let alone the chump change this job was giving me, was, for me, the very definition of what makes a person a ho. At the time I wanted to be a thorough hustler, and you can't be a thorough hustler if you allow people to treat you like a ho.

In my mind, I felt it was bad enough to be in a position where I had to work a janky square job. On top of that, the owners were talking to me like I'm some low budget ho. It was then and there that I made the decision that I was never going to work for anyone ever again. I would rather take my chances getting deeper into the street game before I would subject myself to emasculating office racial politics.

I'm not sure if I would recommend that others adopt the mindset that I had, because at the time I was very young and very fearless. Fearless to the point of recklessness. At that age I could afford to be reckless because I didn't have any major responsibilities, I didn't have extravagant bills, and I didn't have children or other dependents to care for. Any risk I took, no matter how reckless or dangerous, would only impact me.

I try to extract life lessons from every experience. I learned great sales techniques at the telemarketing job, and I learned how to build a rapport with potential customers. I also learned that racial politics in the workplace will most likely occur in any work environment where white people are in charge. The best course of action is to play past those obstacles of racial office politics and hustle around it.

Understanding Your Long-Term Objective

If you are a Black person who chooses to work in a white-run workplace, it is imperative that you are very clear about your ultimate long-term objectives and goals. In these types of environments, you generally have three options:

1. Remain in the same position for years and be content with receiving the same salary you started with.

2. Allow yourself to be subjected to unfair racial politics in order to move up in the company, which means you would be drifting into coon territory.

3. Treat the job as an apprenticeship, where you learn all the game you can from working at the company. Next use that knowledge and expertise to start your own business or become an independent contractor.

Let's break down the different levels of racial politics generally associated with the first two options.

Perpetual Entry Level Racial Politics

Many Black people are relegated to the same position throughout the duration of their employment. In many cases, Black people are content with this arrangement because in their minds they at least get a steady paycheck, and possibly medical and dental benefits.

These jobs are usually menial or lower- to mid-tier positions, where Black employees rarely compete with white employees. For many years, Black people were able to make a decent living and be able to comfortably provide for their families in these types of positions. Racial politics came into play, however, when white employers started to bring in undocumented Hispanic immigrants to replace Black workers.

When these Hispanic workers get these positions, many Black people make the mistake of viewing them as a fellow "minority" group with a shared camaraderie. But Hispanic groups, who for the most part identify as white, also view themselves as being in competition with Black society.

Understanding this current atmosphere, Black people don't have the luxury to remain content with these perpetual entry level positions as they once did in the past.

Advanced Position Racial Politics

There are generally two ways for Black people to get promoted into advanced positions at white dominated offices and firms. One, they have a skill set or level of expertise that is so financially crucial that the white employer would rather elevate a Black person in their company than risk allowing them to become an asset for another company. They don't want the Black person to become a competitor.

This was a tactic used by the famous inventor Thomas Edison. Edison hired a Foundational Black American genius named Lewis Latimer to work for his company. Latimer had already worked for Alexander Graham Bell and contributed to the invention of the telephone.

Latimer later took a job position at the U.S. Electric Lighting Company, which was a rival of Thomas Edison's company. Edison saw Latimer's immense talents and ultimately plucked Latimer away so he could work for The Edison Company, where Latimer contributed to the invention of the modern lightbulb (Clarke, 1985; Stewart, 1986).

Another Black inventor, Granville T. Woods, was also a rival of Edison. Edison took Woods to court multiple times over patent disputes, and Woods won every case (Christopher, 1981; Fouché, 2003). When Edison realized he could not beat Woods in court, he ultimately offered him a position at Edison's company. Woods refused the offer.

These tactics are still used today by white owned companies whenever there is a Black person who has great revenue generating potential. The dominant society understands when they have a golden goose. They make sure to put a Black person in a position where that Black person's expertise will benefit the white company to the fullest extent. There is nothing wrong with Black people being in these types of positions as long as they are fairly compensated for their skills and expertise.

The second way for a Black person to be elevated to a higher, advanced position at a white owned company is to allow themselves to become a tokenized negro. To get elevated in this manner, white employers carefully screen Black people to see who has the most coon potential. They will test the waters by casually bringing up topics pertaining to current racial issues and assess the response the Black person gives.

If you show any discomfort or disagreement with a racial topic they bring up, they might leave you in the same job position indefinitely. They will deliberately keep valuable information away from you because they understand that you can't be trusted not to use this information to benefit yourself and other Black people.

But if these white employers or white supervisors bring up a topic that reflects negatively on Black society and a Black person agrees with them sufficiently, they will often start to elevate and promote that Black person. White supervisors and employers have to make sure that Black person has a certain level of disdain for Black society before they elevate him or her.

When rising through the ranks in certain places of employment, you often gain access and become privy to new information that's rarely available to those in lower positions. White employers want to make sure that any Black person they promote will have enough contempt for Black society that they won't share any valuable information with other Black people.

Part of the power of white supremacy is to withhold valuable information from Black society. White employers will tokenize a Black person and promote them to a higher position, and never worry whether that Black person will use their newly acquired knowledge to benefit significant numbers of other Black people. White employers can also use Black employees like this to "prove" there is diversity in certain job positions.

Often, when Black people are elevated to these token positions, not only are Black people required to carry themselves like coons, but white employers will do daily coon qualification tests to make sure that Black person's allegiance is still to white supremacy.

The 3 Types of Coon Qualification Tests

In many job positions at white owned companies, white supervisors and even white coworkers will often have unofficial Coon Qualification Tests so that they can get a reading on their Black employees. These tests measure the comfort level they should have around certain Black employees.

When white people who believe in white supremacy are only around other white people, they often engage in casual anti-Black racism on a daily basis. They sit around telling nigger jokes and using racial epithets as part of their regular conversations. But when a Black person is around, these suspected white supremacists usually have to censor themselves. This is somewhat uncomfortable for such white coworkers who have to work around Black people. Now they have to walk on eggshells, watch their words and catch themselves before they say something that could be deemed racially offensive.

If they can do a Coon Qualification Test to find a Black person who will co-sign their anti-Black rhetoric, these suspected white supremacist coworkers can breath a sigh of relief and just be themselves. As an added bonus, they can also use the Black person as a shield for their racism. If the suspected white supremacist is saying something racially offensive on the job, and other white people get uncomfortable with it, the suspected white supremacist can simply say "my Black buddy over here agrees with me."

There are many different ways that suspected white supremacist employers and coworkers screen Black employees in order to determine how comfortable they should be around Black employees. There are generally three different Coon Qualification Tests used in places of employment. They are:

1. The Racial Hot Topic Test

As I mentioned earlier, the most common way for non-Black employers or coworkers to assess their Black employees is to bring up hot topics from the news cycle that have racial undertones. They will mention these topics and then evaluate the Black person's response.

In the mid-90s, the most common Racial Hot Topic was the O.J. Simpson trial. Many people in the dominant society would ask a Black person their opinion on the case and the verdict. If the Black person gave an answer that appeared to be in support of the O.J. verdict, these Black people would often find themselves treated negatively or indifferently by their white bosses and coworkers.

Common racial hot topics in the present include conversations about the epidemic of police shootings of unarmed Black people or the protests against anti-Black Racism . White coworkers or employers might ask a Black employee their opinion on NFL players kneeling during the National Anthem, or they might ask them about "looters" (which is a code word for Black people - White people are almost never referred to as looters) during protests.

Many Black employees understand that white people who create these types of social tests are actually telegraphing a message. Black people generally understand what these particular white people want to hear. Some Black people pretend to have reservations about social justice protests because they understand that staying in the good graces of certain white people on the job could result in better positions or pay raises.

A Black person going along with white people's anti-Black racism while knowing the information is false or knowing that they don't agree with the white narrative, is a form of soft cooning. If you are a Black person who voluntarily offers up anti-Black talking points around white people, that is *hard* cooning. When suspected white supremacists get Black people into a space where they are comfortable enough to do some hard cooning, this is when a Black person will most likely be on the fast track to promotion.

2. The Touch Test

Another way certain employers and coworkers try to test Black people on the job is by invading their personal space. Often times this takes the form of being very touchy-feely. Black women in particular, often have to deal with such behavior on the job.

It has become almost a cultural phenomenon for suspected white supremacists to touch Black women's hair. This is a very passive aggressive act. This is a subconscious (and conscious) way to exoticize Black women. By now numerous articles, online videos, news reports, and blogs, document Black women expressing their collective discomfort with white people randomly touching and feeling their hair. White society, in other words, is fully aware of Black women's feelings.

Yet despite this understanding, many white people do it anyway.

Many white employers or coworkers do this because they still have to test Black women in order to monitor their level of approval or discomfort. In this way, white employers can decide if they want to promote the Black woman.

Normally, the Touch Test is primarily inflicted on Black women who wear their natural hair. White people on the job rarely touch Black women's hair if they are wearing weaves or lace fronts. Generally, Black women wearing their hair naturally is viewed as a political statement by white society, especially in places of employment. The bigger and more elaborate a Black woman's natural hairstyle, the more white society begins to perceive it as threatening, at least on a subconscious level.

White supremacists have always seen large, natural hairstyles on Black people as an act of rebellion against white society. This concern goes back to the maroon societies in the Caribbean and Americas during the slavery period. Often, the last thing a white supremacist soldier or enslaver saw before he died was a Black rebel maroon fighter with long hair.

It has always been common for Black rebel fighters to wear dreadlocks or Afros. Oral legends suggest that the very name "dreadlocks" came from white supremacists seeing the long, locked hair of the Black people they encountered and referring to it as "dreadful."

During a British invasion of East Africa in the 19th century, guerrilla rebel warriors were referred to as Fuzzy Wuzzies

(Pizzo, 2007) because they wore their hair in large Afros and other long natural styles, and vowed not to cut their hair until they defeated the British.

In the late 1960s and throughout the 1970s, the natural Afro hairstyle became synonymous with the Black Panthers, Black militants and Black power. The message being sent to white society was that Black people were not going to fully conform to white standards of beauty and acceptance. Today, there are still many cases of Black children being targeted and punished at certain schools for wearing their hair in natural styles.

White supremacist society is hypersensitive to any changes in behavior patterns in Black society. They study Black people on a daily basis to assess the slightest hint of rebellious behavior. So when a Black woman shows up to the job with a natural hairstyle, many suspected white supremacists have to immediately do the Touch Test in order to monitor the reaction of the Black woman when her personal space is violated. If her reaction is hostile, she will have the "Angry Black Woman" stigma placed on her at the job, and people will tread lightly. If the Black woman allows them to touch and pet her hair without showing any signs of reservation or hostility, the suspected white supremacist coworkers and employers will feel more at ease in her presence.

3. The Charity Case Test

Many people in the dominant society like to project their poverty fantasies onto Black people. Systematic white supremacy is measured by the orchestrated levels of social inequality between white society and Black society. White supremacists are most comfortable when they feel that the Black people in their vicinity are more downtrodden and destitute than they are. Black people are the only group whose collective success is deemed threatening by white supremacist society. The global system of white supremacy is based on a vertical racial hierarchy with white society at the top and Black people firmly set at the bottom. Whenever Black people appear to achieve any type of independent success, the dominant society fears that the racial vertical line might possibly turn horizontal.

One thing the dominant society fears is having to exist on an equal plane with Black people. The last thing they want is to compete on an equal footing with Black society. White society is most comfortable knowing, or at least feeling, that Black people are in a regressive, needy state.

One test to see if Black people are in a deprived position is to passively aggressively treat certain Black people as charity cases.

Once again, this occurs primarily in job settings because the workplace is often the only place that many people in the dominant society come into close proximity with Black people. Suspected white supremacists in the workplace use this opportunity to project every stereotype they have about Black people onto their Black coworkers. One of these stereotypes is the image of the downtrodden, hard luck Black person who is in need of a white savior.

These white coworkers will do things like offer leftover food, or hand-me-down clothes to Black people. Many times they do this so they can brag to their friends that they helped an underprivileged negro from the ghetto.

If there is only one token Black person employed in a primarily white work environment, the white people will generally act overly accommodating to the lone Black worker. They will shower that Black employee with gifts and favors, understanding that not only do these favors not relinquish the power dynamics of white supremacy, they in fact work to enforce them. Being overly hospitable to one Black person can also be used as an excuse to prove that white people on the job aren't racist.

If Black people turn down these offers, some of these white coworkers will interpret that as a form of hostility. They will often find ways to undermine the Black employees by projecting the "angry Black person" label on them.

The Three Types of White Coworkers to Be Wary Of

When Black people are employed in predominantly white occupied companies, it's very important that they understand the basic racial politics of that particular workplace.

The one thing Black people have to remember is the system of white supremacy is maintained through codes exchanged among people who want to maintain a racially hierarchical system. Again, this system requires white people on the top and Black people on the bottom. As a result, people in the dominant society are constantly spying on, testing and screening Black people to make sure their status is going to still remain on the bottom.

I discussed earlier how certain Black employees are viewed by co-workers and employers in the dominant society. Now I want to focus on the three types of white coworkers that Black people need to be aware of. These are the people who will try to gather information about Black employees and possibly use this information to undermine them.

1. The Water Cooler Bro

This is the guy who will catch Black employees at the water cooler or on lunch break at the job and engage in overly friendly chatter. The Water Cooler Bro will almost act as if he's your best friend because he is so overly friendly.

In many cases, he will initially try to form a camaraderie with a Black employee by casually using hip hop slang in conversations. These hip-hop slang terms are usually at least five years out of date, and they are usually used out of context. He might say something like, "I went to a wedding reception this weekend and I had on a real jiggy outfit."

Once the Water Cooler Bro feels like he has a good enough office rapport with Black co-workers, in many cases he will then veer into discussions about race. He will do this while presenting a veneer of fake objectivity. He will bring up a racial hot topic such as the protests against racial abuse by the race soldiers employed in law enforcement. If the Black employee appears to support the protesters, the Water Cooler Bro will often pretend to be in agreement. But he will go behind your back and tell other coworkers and even Human Resources that the Black employee seems "militant" and "radical."

The Water Cooler Bro will smile in a Black coworker's face and act like he is that employee's best friend, but he will fish for information in order to sabotage that Black employee. It is important to remember not to give too much information to a Water Cooler Bro. Don't share your opinions on every random topic he brings up. Be as vague and dismissive as possible when the Water Cooler Bro is trying to fish for information about you or your opinions.

2.The Plantation Overseer Supervisor

This isn't the guy who hired the Black employees, but he runs the day-to-day operations of the office. He treats Black employees like diversity hires who only got the job because they somehow took advantage of an Affirmative Action program. Typically, this guy was only hired because the owner of the company is his brother-in-law or because of some other form of nepotism.

At heart, this supervisor knows he is incompetent and only got his position because of nepotism, so he tries to project his own incompetence onto the Black employees. He often makes the Black employees' work environment a living hell.

The main tactic of the Plantation Overseer Supervisor is to find ways to passive aggressively get a rise out of Black employees. He will nitpick every little thing a Black employee is doing on the job. He will go out of his way to critique or dismiss the hard work of the Black employee.

The Plantation Overseer Supervisor fully understands that constantly prodding and provoking employees on a daily basis will ultimately frustrate them to the point where they quit or lash out. This is exactly what he wants. These types of suspected white supremacists take pride in coming up with sinister ways to get Black employees fired. In many cases they want to open up a job position for one of their white cronies. In other cases they just get a power rush from knowing that the system of white supremacy allows them the privilege to negatively impact the lives of Black people.

Another tactic the Plantation Overseer Supervisor will use is to drop slick little racially coded comments around Black employees. He will get around Black employees and purposely make comments about "thugs in Chicago" or people on "welfare in the ghetto." He will keep using these racially coded insults in the hope that a Black employee will ultimately get fed up and possibly threaten or even assault him. He will use an incident like that to file criminal charges against the Black employee and then try and sue the company.

When dealing with a Plantation Overseer type on the job, it's very important not to take his bait or react emotionally to his racial antagonism. Stay cool, and if you are able to, simply record everything he says to you. You have to think ten steps ahead of these Plantation Overseer Supervisor types. These people are constantly in a battle against you and it's important to hold a trump card against them if needs be.

If you secretly record them engaging in racially insensitive or derogatory conversations, you can use that recording against the suspected white supremacist. You can take the recording down to the Human Resources department and possibly get the supervisor fired. You can also use the recording to file a possible lawsuit against the supervisor and the company. Always use the antagonism of the Plantation Overseer Supervisor to *your* advantage.

3. The Interrogating Karen

This is the suspected white supremacist female at your job who is constantly trying to get information about your job position and personal life. The Interrogating Karen will move around the office inquiring about the salaries and promotion status of Black employees.

The Interrogating Karen interacts with Black male and Black female employees in slightly different ways. With Black male employees, the Karen will often create the mental façade that the Black man in the office is somehow desirous of her. No matter how old or haggard she might be, in many cases the Interrogating Karen will tell her friends and other coworkers that the Black men at her job are somehow interested in her sexually. This is usually a fetish or desire that she is projecting. By projecting this narrative, the Karen can claim that any kind of interaction with a Black male employee is some form of sexual harassment.

There is a long tradition in white supremacist society of white women falsely accusing Black men of sexual improprieties. Over the years, certain legal terms have been introduced to create a legal precedent for these types of claims.

If a Black man looks at a Karen for a few seconds too long, the Karen can claim the Black man was "leering" at her. If a Black man walks past a Karen in the hallway and his arm brushes against hers, the Karen can claim she was "groped." If a Black man walks into an area at work where a Karen is working, and the Black man doesn't say anything, the Karen can accuse the Black man of "menacing" her. If a Black male employee innocently compliments a Karen's coat or shoes, the Karen can accuse the Black man of making "sexually suggestive" comments.

Some of these scenarios might sound like exaggerations, but many of these things have actually happened in high profile incidents involving Black male entertainers. In 2018, sexual harassment charges were filed against the actor Morgan Freeman by several women he associated with in the media. Some of the accusations were things like "staring" at women and staring at their breasts, and "sexually suggestive comments."

Black American businessman and former athlete LaVar Ball appeared on the sports network ESPN to discuss game commentary with the hosts. A white female host named Molly Qerim asked LaVar, "can I switch gears with you?" LaVar innocently responded, "you can switch gears with me anytime."

The female co-host and the ESPN network invoked the "I'm white and I say so" principle and interpreted LaVar Ball's comment as somehow sexual. He was then banned from coming back on the network.

When working or doing business in a white dominated/controlled environment, Black people and Black men in particular have to be very aware of the "I'm white and I say so" rule, which can be invoked against unsuspecting Black people at any moment. Part of white supremacist culture is lying on Black people and deliberately making false accusations to justify using the system to punish them.

The Interrogating Karen engages in a different set of tactics against Black women on the job. She interjects herself into Black women's personal business, almost to the point of harassment. Karens who work around Black women always have to assure themselves that Black women on the job are socially beneath them. The Karens have to constantly monitor Black women who seem to get any type of preferential treatment over them on the job.

If a Black woman is considered to be overweight or homely according to the standards of white supremacist society, the Karens fully embrace her. As long as these Karens view Black women as Mammy-type figures, they have no problem with them. But if there is a relatively attractive Black woman at the office, often the Karens will feel threatened. Interrogating Karens will often make it their mission to monitor these Black women daily.

The Karens will take notice of every new purse, item of clothing, or hairstyle that Black women show up to work with. They will then mask their interrogation under the guise of compliments. They will say something like, "Hey Kendra, that's a lovely new purse you have." And then slip in something like, "How much did it cost?"

If the Karen's finds out that the purse or articles of clothing are just a little too expensive for the Black woman's perceived salary, the Karen will low-key take issue. She will smile to the Black woman's face, then go behind her back to management and make the same type of accusatory Affirmative Action claims as the Plantation Overseer Supervisor.

The Interrogating Karen will constantly ask Black women at the job about their salaries, raises, promotions or any other perks to which the Karen feels entitled. The Interrogating Karens will also monitor Black women's social media and inquire about vacation photos or other activities that appear to be expensive.

These Karens like to view Black women as downtrodden and poverty stricken. This makes them comfortable in their white supremacist ideologies. In a system of white supremacy, if a suspected white supremacist isn't doing better than the Black people in their daily lives, then what's the point in having the system of racial injustice?

The moment it appears that a Black woman is being treated equally, the Interrogating Karen goes on the alert. If the Karen finds out a Black woman is excelling or progressing over her at the job, the Karen goes into sabotage mode.

Certain Karens will report bogus claims and accusations about Black women to Human Resources. They will make complaints to management about Black women's work attire.

They will make passive aggressive remarks to Black women, and if Black women check them on it, the Karens will go into victim mode and tell management that they were attacked. If a Black woman on the job chooses not to engage the Interrogating Karen and her shenanigans, the Karen will complain to her supervisors that the Black woman is acting "angry."

When dealing with an Interrogating Karen type on your job, always try to be as vague as possible when they're trying to get your personal information. You have to deal with the Karens the same way you deal with the police: understand that everything you say to them can be used against you. Try to keep your interactions with Interrogating Karens cordial but as brief as possible.

When the Karen tries to trigger you with passive aggressive comments, do not take the bait. They want you to have an emotional reaction to them so they can turn around and get you reprimanded or fired from the job.

The Four Types of Black Employees Suspected Racists Prefer On the Job

I have provided an assessment of the main types of suspected racists that Black people may encounter in the workplace. I have also analyzed the type of Black people these suspected racists are cautious around. Now we will look at the four types of Black employees that suspected racists are most comfortable with in the workplace.

It's important to understand these four types, because all four have to compromise their integrity on a daily basis. After a while, this becomes stressful. If you allow your integrity to be constantly compromised, eventually your spirit will be broken. White supremacists love it when they have Black people around who they have spiritually and mentally broken. They understand that these Black people are not a threat and are less likely to rebel against them.

1. The Office Mammy

Suspected white supremacists in job situations love the jovial mammy type of Black woman in the workplace. The Mammy type at the job is usually an older and/or overweight woman who has a maternal, non-threatening disposition around white coworkers.

Generally, white male managers and supervisors like the office Mammy because she often keeps the other Black people in the office in line. White women like the office Mammy because she is generally not perceived to be sexual competition.

The Office Mammy does things like bring homemade baked goods to work to share with white coworkers. She also goes around the office hugging on white coworkers and praying for them. The white bosses at the job will give the Office Mammy little token positions, with meaningless but distinguished sounding titles, such as Advisory Director or Communications Manager.

This same dynamic was at work during antebellum slavery. Women classified as mammies were allowed in the big house, and their disposition had to generally be jovial and all-caring for the white slave owner's family.

Today, the Office Mammy is given the illusion of importance so that the white bosses at the job can use her to report on the activities of the other Black employees. She will often-times skin and grin around other Black employees, while go-ing overboard with the "sista-girl" act. She will do this to lower their defenses so she can get intel to report back to the white management or to Human Resources.

In many cases, when a Black person is written up at work for some type of insubordination, or if they are fired from the job, this is a result of the Office Mammy snitching on them to management.

2. The Plantation Uncle

This is usually a middle-aged or elderly Black man working at a company or institution where he is in a lower position than most of the white employees. He is usually the door-man, the shoe shine man, the security guard or the janitor.

Since his job position is not in competition with the white employees, the Plantation Uncle often becomes the best buddy of the white employees. Not only do the white employees go out of their way to be extra friendly to the Plantation Uncle, they often shower him with gifts and good-ies.

White employees bring food, presents, sports tickets, and other treats to the job to give to their best Black friend the

Plantation Uncle. This is a subliminal way to reward him for accepting his subservient position.

Because the Plantation Uncle is usually older and beyond his sexual prime, he is viewed as non-threatening to white society. The Plantation Uncle is not in sexual competition with white men and he is not perceived as a sexual menace to the white women. He is viewed as a sort of asexual and harmless family pet.

Old movies commonly showcased this dynamic in films like *Song of the South*, a racist Disney musical that featured a former slave character named Uncle Remus. It was released in 1946 at the height of the Hays Code, a code and policy of the motion picture industry that explicitly forbade the depiction of miscegenation in films, which it defined as "sex relationships between the white and black races" (Reed, 1998).

A Black man and white woman appearing together on screen in any capacity that represented equality was a major no-no at the time. *Song of the South* represented the exception to this rule as the older, subservient Black man shared the screen with little white children, particularly little white girls.

Throughout *Song of the South*, the lead character Uncle Remus happily shuffled around, hand in hand, with a white boy and white girl. Other films of the same era frequently featured an older Black "uncle" figure, like Mr. Bojangles tap dancing in scenes with the white female child star Shirley Temple. Two things were accomplished with this particular dynamic.

One, it allowed Black men and white women to interact on-screen as long as the Black male was sexually non-threatening and past his sexual prime due to his age.

Second, by constantly contrasting older Black men alongside white female children, this projected a deeper message: the older Black man was still considered a "boy" who was equal to a white child but not to a white adult.

The Plantation Uncle in the workplace is seen in the same manner. White coworkers view him as an old harmless child. He is almost viewed as a member of their family, as long as he remains in a subordinate job position under his white coworkers.

When a Plantation Uncle, or any other Black man in the workplace, gets promoted from the mailroom, the security desk, or any other subordinate job position, and begins to rise in the ranks, then he becomes a problem. The more competitive Black people become with white employees, the friendly banter starts to disappear. If by chance a Plantation Uncle gets promoted to supervisor or any other position of seniority over the white employees, the previous laughter and joking with white employees often turns into outright hostility.

In many cases, this is when all types of frivolous accusations against the Black man, initially perceived as a harmless Plantation Uncle, start. White male employees might accuse him of reverse racism, while white female employees will start filing sexual misconduct allegations against him.

3. Immigrant Coons

White supremacists understand Black people almost better than Black people understand themselves. Going back to slavery in the Western Hemisphere, they understood the importance and the science of using certain Black people from different areas and tribal groups to carry out certain tasks. White supremacists realized that having too many enslaved Black people from the same area or ethnic group would mean the Black captives would have their own code of conduct. This meant they could better organize rebellions.

Slave rebellions were more frequent on the Caribbean islands because the slave traders often brought in Black people from the same region in Africa. This differed from the way slave owners dealt with Black people in North America. In North America, Black people were purchased in smaller quantities by individual slave owners. After they were purchased, they were usually scattered and sent to far off regions around the country. These enslaved Black people would be brought among other enslaved Foundational Black Americans who already had deeply rooted ancestry in America. So communication and the ability to share a code with each other proved more of a challenge.

In the Caribbean, however, as the land masses were smaller, enslaved Black people had easier access to correspond and plan with other Black people. Because many came from the same general region of Africa, they were in a better position to communicate with each other. They would use drums to send secret signals to the other side of the islands when it was time to revolt. Ultimately, many British slave owners caught on to what was happening and they banned drums from certain islands (Manuel, Bilpy et al., 2012; Rath, 2001).

In Haiti, the most successful slave revolt in history was carried out against three white supremacist military superpowers at the time, France, Spain and Britain. One of the reasons Black people in Haiti were able to succeed was because many of them were able to maintain a cultural and spiritual continuity with their previous lives in Africa.

White supremacists quickly learned from this defeat and they put their heads together to come up with ways to prevent these types of threats to their systematic dominance. They learned to create buffer classes within Black society. Since all Black people had the same victim status under white supremacy, white supremacists learned to create differences based on skin shade and on ethnic and tribal differences.

By giving certain Black ethnic groups extra rations within the societal confines of the global prison of white supremacy, the dominant society learned how to better control the Black masses. Fast forward to the present, this context and dynamic have been applied to the workplace.

White supremacist society in America has always viewed Foundational Black Americans as an intrinsic threat. Foundational Black Americans are the only group on the planet that has consistently challenged and resisted white supremacy for 500 years. Even before Foundational Black Americans built what would become the United States, we were fighting white supremacy.

White supremacists understand that if they provoke or antagonize us for too long, FBA can flip on them when they least expect it. They know that FBA are not as eager to go along and accept the types of casual racism that suspected white supremacists often engage in at the workplace. Thus, white supremacists often prefer to hire Black people with foreign backgrounds for certain job positions.

Even though they overtly deny this, white supremacist society understands that they owe Foundational Black Americans for building the country's wealth generated from free labor during antebellum slavery. They also understand that they owe Foundational Black Americans for all the atrocities they committed during the Jim Crow era. And they understand, if just on a subconscious level, that they owe Black people some form of compensation for the anti-Black war that has been waged on Black American society over the recent decades.

White America doesn't owe Black people from immigrant backgrounds anything. Many immigrants, including first, second, and third generation immigrants, are simply grateful to have the opportunity to be in America and to benefit from the opportunities that Foundational Black Americans help make possible for them. These people from immigrant backgrounds are more likely to go out of their way not to rock the boat or complain about racial mistreatment. This allows white Americans to be more comfortable around them as compared to Foundational Black Americans.

White supremacists often make sure that if they bring Black immigrants into the workplace, they get them specifically from the coon class of foreign society. White Americans are very careful not to allow more revolutionarily minded Black people from Africa and the Caribbean to be around Foundational Black Americans. The last thing they want is another Marcus Garvey situation where Black people start building a globally targeted code of conduct.

White supremacists like to pull foreign Black people to the side and tell them how they like them so much better than Black Americans. This is a divide and conquer con-game that white supremacists have been running since the 1970s. Before that, it was white supremacists who implemented strict immigration quotas that kept most foreign Black people out of the United States (Muller, 1994; Ngai, 1999). It was Foundational Black Americans who fought for immigration laws that allowed foreign Black people to come to the U.S. in significant numbers.

Many non-FBA immigrants start to buy into the model minority con-game that the white supremacists run on them. Many people with an immigrant lineage willingly allow themselves to become part of a buffer class for white supremacy. As a buffer, they realize that it's their duty to undermine FBA.

White supremacists prefer to have this buffer-class sector around because they aren't going to challenge white supremacy and they are going to generally keep their distance from FBA employees.

4.The Broken Buck

As I stated earlier, during antebellum slavery, one tactic used by white slave owners to subdue and break the spirit of an enslaved Black male was to sexually assault him. Stories about enslaved Black women are commonly known because of the mulatto offspring that stemmed from such encounters. But stories about the sexual assault of Black men during slavery are still seen as taboo. However, recollections and stories about these assaults have been passed down through the oral tradition.

In modern times, the sexual abuse and exploitation of Black men, especially at the hands of white supremacist society, is something that is not openly discussed. There are countless cases where Black children are adopted by white people and because of unchecked sexual abuse, the Black child grows up with issues of sexual confusion.

The sexual exploitation and "breaking" of Black men is almost ritualistic for the white supremacist. White supremacists seem to get a thrill out of emasculating Black men. White supremacist society understands that the main people who challenge and fight systematic white supremacy, are Black people, and Black men in particular.

White supremacists feel it is in their best interests to come up with socially manipulative tactics to confuse Black men sexually. If you can manipulate and control a person sexually, you can easily control them in other areas.

This includes the workplace.

In the workplace, suspected white supremacist men like to make sure the optics of the racial hierarchy are presented in their favor. They want to be seen as the alpha males. This is especially true if women are employed at the same establishment.

Heterosexual Black men in the workplace are a threat to the optics of the racial hierarchy because straight Black men are generally viewed as the epitome of masculinity. In many major white owned companies, when straight Black men are hired they are usually relegated to menial or laborer positions, far away from the white female employees at the company.

When Black men are put in an equal position with their white coworkers, the white employers will generally try to hire a non-heterosexual Black man for that position. White employers assume that the non-heterosexual Black man is already buck broken, and he won't go against the grain too much.

Oftentimes, white employers, as well as white employees, get a kick out of having a non-heterosexual Black man running around the workplace. These men are often viewed as social eunuchs who don't threaten the power dynamics of the racial hierarchy at the job.

White people on the job will often view this type of Black man as a broken buck who they can tokenize. They shower the broken buck with gifts and preferential treatment, and treat him like a social mascot.

The Broken Buck will be treated like the life of the party in social settings involving his white coworkers. They have no problem parading him around because in their minds the Broken Buck does not pose a sexual threat to white women.

Further, the Broken Buck isn't perceived to be competition for white men in the workplace. In fact, some Broken Bucks offer sexual companionship to white men. It is this type of Black man that white employers are most comfortable with allowing into their work and social spaces.

Racially Targeted Exclusion

Many Black people are subjected to racial workplace politics even before they get a job. In the process of seeking employment, Black people have to deal with racial discrimination and racially exclusionary games played by white companies.

It is imperative for Black people to understand these racial games so that Black people don't take these white supremacist tactics personally when they experience them.

White supremacists have mastered the art of coming up with discriminatory tactics that they can use to get around civil rights discrimination laws. **Here are three common tactics that white supremacist employers use to deny qualified Black people employment opportunities:**

1. Name discrimination

This is one of the most common forms of employment discrimination against Black people. Many studies and reports have documented how white employers will look at an application, see a name that appears to be "Black", and then throw these applications out (Jacquemet, 2012; Turner et al., 1991).

A Black person could be overqualified for the position, but that is irrelevant. A white employer who doesn't want to hire a Black person in the first place, feels like their job is easier once they see a Black sounding name. They will just toss the Black person's application and be done with it.

2. Unions

There is a long history of labor unions being used to discriminate and exclude Black people from jobs. After formal slavery, the former enslaved Black people had a competitive advantage over white workers in the job market. Black people were the most skilled laborers across the board. During formal slavery, Black people were made to utilize all their skills and trades without compensation.

With the end of formal slavery. Black people were allowed to participate in the paid employment market. This was viewed as a problem. Black people were coming out of slavery with so many valuable skill sets that they immediately began to dominate certain industries and gain an economic footing. White supremacist society had to come up with ways to thwart the progress of Black society. Right after Reconstruction, the American government opened its borders and allowed all types of Europeans immigrants from the slums of their home countries to flood the United States. This was done to undermine the newly freed Foundational Black Americans. These European immigrants were deliberately elevated over Black people in the job markets, and these immigrants became involved with racially exclusionary labor unions.

One of the earliest and largest labor unions formed at the tail end of the 19th century was the American Federation of Labor, led by British immigrant Samuel Gompers. The AFL went out of its way to discriminate against Foundational Black American workers (Jones, 2013; Quadagno, 1994). This tradition of anti-Black discrimination within white run unions remains prevalent today.

3.Phony Aptitude Tests

Another way that some jobs racially discriminate is requiring applicants to take loaded aptitude tests. This technique's purpose is to force applicants to take extremely difficult tests that usually have little or nothing to do with the job position. If a Black applicant happens to fail one of these tests, suspected white supremacist employers can deny that their decision not to hire the Black person was because of race. The employers can say that they didn't hire a certain Black person, not because of racial bias, but because they simply weren't smart enough to pass the test.

Something like this happened in a well-publicized story out of New York City. In 2014 the NY Fire Department agreed to a $98 million dollar settlement with a group of Black men and some others who were discriminated against. These men claimed they were made to take a test that was deliberately deceptive. According to the judge who presided over the case, the written tests had "discriminatory effects and little relationship to the job of a firefighter." The judge also concluded that the "examinations unfairly excluded hundreds of qualified people of color from the opportunity to serve as New York City firefighters."

This type of Phony Aptitude Test tactic is common at many jobs. The white employer will give applicants a questionable test, and the Black applicants are stumped. However, because so many white employees are grandfathered in, especially in fire department jobs and similar positions, the answers to these " tests" are known to them in advance. So many of these positions are passed down generationally through family members, who look out for each other.

Another variation on this form of racial discrimination is to require certain "certificates" or licenses for certain job positions. Just like many other positions, white applicants are often grandfathered in and they either bypass the certification requirements or are given the answers for the certification exams in advance. Black applicants are made to jump through all types of hoops in order to get certification documents for a job position, and when Black applicants fail, plausible deniability of racism has already been established. Denial of employment can be attributed to lack of aptitude.

If these tactics are reminiscent of the Literacy Tests that Black voters faced during the Jim Crow era, it's not a coincidence. In order to restrict Black people's right to vote, white supremacists employed all types of sabotage tactics. Violence and lynching were first used to deter Black people from voting, but soon they moved on to more covert tactics such as literacy tests.

Many of these tests would ask arbitrary questions that were almost impossible for the average layman to comprehend, such as "can you be imprisoned under Alabama law for debt?" In some states, the literacy tests were worded in a deliberately confusing manner so the white registrar who administered the test could use, at his discretion, the "I'm white and I say so" rule to decide whether the answers were correct. White people were generally not subjected to these tests. Whenever they were required to take these tests, in order to maintain the illusion of racial fairness, the answers to these deliberately vague questions would be marked as correct.

This culture of codified cheating is common in white supremacist culture. A few years ago, a group of white Hollywood actresses were caught in an elaborate college cheating scandal. An entire network of white people were on-code working with each other to fraudulently allow the parents of unqualified white students to buy spots for their children at elite universities.

This shameless cheating mentality dominates all other areas of white supremacist society. When they are in competition with Black people, they always have to unfairly stack the deck in their favor. White supremacists view themselves as being at constant war with Black people. And all is fair in war, even cheating.

CHAPTER SEVEN

Perceived Allies

As a kid growing up in the 70s, I loved going to see Asian Kung Fu movies. During the 70s, a white flight wave occurred across the United States in response to the perceived Black gains from the Civil Rights movement. Many urban areas that Black people moved into were abandoned by whites who started to flock to newly formed suburbs.

Consequently, movie theaters in these urban areas took a financial hit because of white flight. The entire Hollywood movie system took a loss as well. In order for many large downtown movie theaters to survive during this period, they had to show XXX-rated films, Blaxploitation films or cheap martial arts films bought from China, particularly Hong Kong.

Movie theaters at the time had developed a new Black audience. In order to keep the audiences in the theaters as long as possible, so that the theater could rack up on concession money, they would often have triple feature film showings.

I remember going to these theaters as a kid and paying two or three bucks to watch triple feature Black action and Asian Kung Fu films all day. This was common for many Black youths during this era. Many of the Black themed films at the time, even the exploitation films, always seemed to carry a message of Black empowerment. Studios were aware that they were pandering to a predominantly Black audience, so these films would always feature a "get whitey" retributive dynamic.

The retaliatory nature of Blaxploitation films allowed Black audiences to feel a sense of justice against systematic racism through using these movies as a proxy. Asian martial arts movies had a similar theme with which urban Black audiences identified. Martial arts movies usually featured a theme where the lead character was an underdog figure fighting against a larger oppressive system. Many of these films had the Asian lead fighting a white villain or opponent.

From the perspective of Foundational Black American youths, when we saw these 70s Kung fu films we felt a kinship with the characters we perceived to be fellow oppressed non-white minorities. Many Black youths throughout that period idolized people like Bruce Lee. As a kid I remember being a big fan of Jackie Chan because of his early movies.

Because Foundational Black Americans have dealt with and rebelled against systematic white supremacy for 500 years, we have a general fighting spirit when it comes to non-justice. We gravitated towards those 70s martial arts movies because we could identify with the perceived fighting spirit of the Asian actors.

At the same time the Vietnam War was still ongoing, and every night on the news there were images of Asian soldiers successfully defending themselves from the mightiest military operation in the world. Black people were just coming out of the Civil Rights movement, so we identified our struggle with the perceived struggles of other "people of color."

Starting in the late 1960s and throughout the 70s, Foundational Black Americans fought for non-white immigrant groups to come to the United States. Foundational Black American icons such as Muhammad Ali risked his career and freedom when he famously refused to go fight in Vietnam.

Other Foundational Black American freedom fighters in the 1960s like Robert F. Williams traveled to Asia after he went into exile when he got word that false charges that were going to be levied against him. Williams showed solidarity with China and Vietnam during the Vietnam War while in exile.

The Black Panther Party and one of its leaders, Huey P. Newton, also showed solidarity with Vietnam. He became such a staunch ally that the North Vietnamese government offered to release Americans POWs if the U.S. government freed imprisoned members of the Black Panthers (Bloom, 2016; Hershberger, 1998).

Black Americans saw engagements like this with Asians throughout the 60s and 70s and assumed we would have a lifelong alliance with them. But many of these Asian societies, in the United States and abroad, understood the importance of having temporary allies when it was beneficial. Black people, on the other hand, have a history of remaining loyal to other groups, to a fault.

When Allies Become Adversaries

Many non-Foundational Black American ethnic groups will act as allies to FBA when it's convenient and then turn around and become violent adversaries when it benefits them. Other groups understand the importance of looking out for the best interests of their particular group, first.

Going back to the 1970s, Black people embraced Asian art forms and Black people embraced Asian immigrants who came to the United States in droves. Many of these Asian immigrants came to the U.S., got access to capital, and opened up businesses. And unlike the experience of Black people, these Asian businesses were not repeatedly sabotaged by the dominant society.

Black people have been programmed to view themselves as part of some larger, mythical minority coalition, where all these non-white people are looking out for each other's best interests. When Asian businesses set up in Black neighborhoods, Black residents had no issues patronizing these establishments. In cities around the country, the Foundational

Black American community became the economic base for these Asian businesses.

Black people did not realize that these perceived allies were morphing into economic adversaries. The assumed allyship was extremely one-sided, as is the case with most perceived coalitions with Foundational Black Americans. The Asian community benefited from 1965 Immigration Bill that Foundational Black Americans fought to push through. The Asian community benefitted from the "minority" set aside programs and policies that Foundational Black Americans pushed for. And they benefitted from the direct capital they received from Black people supporting their businesses. In many cases, Black people were the exclusive customer base for Asian-run businesses.

After the 1960s, when Black people were duped into giving up many of their businesses in the name of integration, many did not understand what the term integration meant. During the Jim Crow era, Black people were subject to open segregation laws. Segregation is just another form of white supremacy. The most productive way for Black people to counter systematic white supremacy is to create a protective cultural and military system grounded on a solid economic base. But Black people thought the antithesis to segregation was integration.

Unlike economic resources, integration is an unquantifiable ideology. The dominant society had no problem implementing integration policies in order to pacify Black people. White society did not have to relinquish any significant economic power to Black society. Black people, however, were bamboozled into relinquishing their economic base. The only thing so-called integration allowed, was for Black people to spend their money in white and non-Black establishments, and have sexual access to white people.

Being able to patronize businesses in the dominant society gave Black people the illusion of allyship and acceptance. But this was another one-sided coalition that financially strengthened white communities and weakened the Black community. White society has always viewed Black society as an adversarial group that must be dominated and crippled to the point where they are non-competitive. The Asian community typically views Black society in the same way.

In white supremacist circles, Asians are often seen as "honorary Aryans." Even if white supremacist society and certain parts of Asian society are in competition or even at war with each other, they both still get on-code when it comes to dominating Black people.

While certain parts of Asian society were at war with the white military superpowers in the 1960s, some Asian countries allied with people in the Black power movement in America, as stated earlier. Once these Asian societies achieved peace with the white superpowers, they immigrated to the United States and ultimately allied with white society, slowly becoming adversaries of Black society.

None of the money Asian immigrants accumulated from their Black customer base trickled back into Black communities. The Asian community, for the most part, did not patronize the few Black-owned businesses that survived. Other than a merchant/customer relationship, the Asian community did not and still does not have any significant business dealings with Black people.

Like other immigrant groups that Foundational Black Americans helped to stabilize in the United States, the Asian community got their resources in order and became economic adversaries to Black society. When a group accepts a certain level of domination from another group, more hostile forms of contempt soon follow.

Black people have naively assumed that Asians view themselves as another oppressed minority group similar to Black people. The reality is that many Asians see themselves as being closer to European society. From a historic and geographic standpoint, they share the Eurasian landmass with white people. Now they are ranked higher on the racial totem pole of white society.

It is generally understood that the global racial hierarchy constructed by white supremacists is ranked as follows, from the most socially important to the most socially powerless:

1. Whites
2. Asians
3. Arabs
4. Hispanics
5. Blacks

On this list some notable "races" are left out. Many dark skinned East Indians, Australian Aborigines, Micronesians and Polynesians are considered Black by white supremacist society. I did not include Native Americans because most have been absorbed into Black society, or some have been coopted by white society. Most Foundational Black Americans have native Black Aboriginal American heritage because the original people of America were Black skinned people.

Because many people in Asian society see themselves as sharing a closer camaraderie with white society, they often participate in cultural anti-Blackness as a way to show their allegiance to white society.

We see the results of this today with the aggressive presence of Asians who are dominating the economy in parts of Africa and the Caribbean. In America today, we often see violent and hostile incidents between some Asian merchants at beauty supply stores and nail salons that have Black customers.

We also witnessed incidents like the infamous case of an Asian New York police officer named Peter Liang who was spared jail time after he killed an innocent Black man. Thousands of Asians all over the country protested for Peter Liang's freedom. While Black people are desperately trying to pretend that there is a minority coalition, the Asian community collectively got on-code against Black people and are unapologetic about it.

The Five Types of Historically Deceptive White Allies

Historically, many white liberals have deceived Black people into believing they are true allies. They often point to the more open racism of white conservatives to portray themselves as different. Even though there are white liberals, as well as white conservatives, who are genuine in their outreach or assistance to Black people and Black causes, these white people are not the majority in power. If they were, we would not have systematic white supremacy dominating the planet.

1. Political Operatives

These are the white liberal elected officials or employees of political parties who go around Black people during election season to pander for votes. They usually show up to HBCUs or Black churches, pretending to care about Black culture, in order to win Black people over. They never ask Black people what the community wants because they usually come in with their own agenda that they try to sell Black people on.

White political operatives usually try to push a one-sided minority coalition where they can neglect Black issues. They hide this neglect under the illusion of assumed minority benefits that will eventually trickle down to Black people.

These political operatives pretend to be allies to Black people by listening to them tell their stories about suffering and discrimination. White society understands that a lot of Black people are satisfied with just getting some attention from white people. Often, this fake ally pandering alone will suffice for many Black people.

After Black people vote these political operatives or their party into office, these politicians go back to ignoring Black people and their issues for another four years.

2. Swirlers

Swirlers are white people who have a fetish for sexually swirling with Black people. Swirling is a reference to chocolate and vanilla ice cream mixed together on a cone to form a "swirl." Many white people who sexually swirl with Black people still retain anti-Black views and ideologies. Many Black people are confused by this dichotomy. Black people will often let their defenses down around white people with whom they are having sexual relations.

White swirlers use Black people's sexual/social confusion to their advantage. Many times, these white swirlers like to present themselves as allies to Black people and Black causes. However, they will often use their sexual arrangement with Black people as a cloak to cover their own racism.

Many of these white swirlers will engage in what Neely Fuller calls racial showcasing. They will go out of their way to make a public display of their involvement with a Black person. They will go overboard with public displays of affection when they are out with a Black person with whom they are sexually involved. Sometimes they will do this to the point of lewdness, especially in the case of white male swirlers involved with Black women. In 2014, Daniele Watts, a Black actress who appeared in the film *Django Unchained*, was arrested in Los Angeles after she and her white boyfriend were allegedly spotted having sex in broad daylight in their parked car on a busy street.

Racial showcasing like this is something that many white swirlers do to appear edgy and eccentric. These types of arrangements become more like social or political statements than genuine loving relationships. Many white swirlers have YouTube channels that center around their "interracial relationships." All this showboating is designed to create the illusion that anti-Black racism no longer exists in the same way it did in the past.

3. White Feminists

White women in the first and second wave feminist movements have always pretended to be allies with Black people and Black women in particular. They have done this as a Trojan horse to advance their own agenda where white women accumulate tangibles for themselves.

In the first wave of feminism, many of the notable white women who were at the forefront of the movement started out as abolitionists. That was a hustle in and of itself, because many white abolitionists were not interested in real equality for Black people. White abolitionists were using the plight of Black people to collect money and donations for themselves. The same is true today with white-backed "Black" social justice organizations. These organizations exploit the deaths of Black people to raise money for themselves, and the Black masses and even Black victims of white supremacist injustice never see the money.

It was necessary for first wave of white feminists to latch onto the struggles of Black people because white women had no comparative struggle. In fact, white supremacist women were 50/50 partners with white supremacist men in reaping the benefits of the racial domination and exploitation of Black people. It would have been a hard sell to convince the public that white women were oppressed in any way comparable to Black people when so many white supremacist women acted as oppressor.

Early white feminists like Susan B. Anthony and Elizabeth Cady Stanton latched onto Black people like Sojourner Truth and Frederick Douglas (Dapena Barba; Thomas, 2016), using them as Trojan horses for their white feminist agenda. When these white women realized that Black men were going to get the vote before white women, Susan B. Anthony and other white feminists dropped the fake ally shtick and put their anti-Black racism on full display. Susan B. Anthony infamously stated, "I will cut off this right arm of mine before I will ever work or demand the ballot for the Negro and not the woman."

Many first wave white feminists became infamous for their anti-Black rhetoric. Hundreds, if not thousands, of Black men were lynched because of the white supremacist propaganda that white feminists were spewing. When we fast forward to today, white feminists tried to make Black men the face of the Me Too Movement, while they pretend to be allies with Black women. The reality is, white feminists have never helped Black women and they have done nothing to help Black society. All they have done is use fake ally propaganda to exploit Black people for their own benefit.

4. Hipsters

The general perception of a hipster is a liberal white person who follows the latest trends and fashions, especially those regarded to be outside the cultural mainstream. Black people are collectively viewed as an out-group that is marginalized from mainstream society. As such, the white hipster's association with anything that is considered Black culture makes them seem more hip.

Many white hipsters appear to be allied with Black people because they will often frequent areas or involve themselves in activities associated with Black society. White hipsters might go to hip hop clubs or concerts, soul food restaurants, or poetry slams. They will also engage in more seedy activities when they get around Black people. They might come around Black people to purchase or use drugs, or they might frequent Black strip clubs, and so on. In the early twentieth century this type of behavior was called "slumming." During the height of Jim Crow segregation, Black people would get lynched for wandering anywhere near a white neighborhood, but white people could frequent the Red Light Districts of Black areas on a regular basis to indulge their vices.

Today, many white hipsters participate in racial justice protests, and this further gives the illusion of allyship. These white liberals have no problem marching around the streets with Black people for a few hours to chant about police brutality because when these protests are over these white liberals go back to their segregated white neighborhoods, and Black people have to remain in the areas under militarized police occupation.

Many Black people often ask why these white hipster allies, who show up to protests with Black people by the thousands, are almost never on the jury pools when it comes to convicting white police officers who murder Black people? The reality is that many of these so-called liberal white people *are* on these jury pools where they allow police to commit racial murder with impunity. These same white people will leave the jury box after they have acquitted a white race soldier for murdering a Black person, and go into the street and march hand in hand with Black people against police violence.

White hipsters are also the main gentrifiers of Black neighborhoods. Hipsters will trickle into Black areas one by one. Some will even hang out with a few Black people to smoke weed, share drinks and party. This will go on for a few years, but that friendly, ally façade will disappear once these hipsters start to have children. White people generally do not want their white children to go to school with Black children. Black people will suddenly see their white hipster allies become more and more hostile to their presence when white children come into the picture.

Many of the white "Karen" videos that we see circulating online, where hostile white women harass Black people, come from areas where white hipsters are gentrifying Black neighborhoods. One infamous case from St. Louis saw some Black Lives Matter protesters march into a gated community. A white couple ran outside and pointed guns at them. The couple, who were both lawyers, would later claim they have always supported Black Lives Matter and fought for Civil Rights.

When these white hipsters reach the age where they start having families, we normally see a rise in anti-Black harassment. These same hipsters will call the police on Black people for trivial reasons. They will generally target and antagonize Black people in an effort to frustrate the Black residents so that they will eventually leave.

5.White LGBT

The white LGBT community has historically maintained a very exploitive association with Black people. Many people in the white LGBT community practice the same anti-Black racism as the rest of the dominant society.

There have been written and oral narratives passed down since antebellum slavery about gay white slave owners who would sexually violate Black male slaves. There were prominent open and closeted white LGBT people like J. Edgar Hoover who waged a domestic war against Black society.

Alleged criminals like Ed Buck and convicted serial killers in the white LGBT community like Jeffrey Dahmer and Ronald Dominique have all primarily targeted Black men as their victims.

The white LGBT community also practices discriminatory policies against Black gay people at nightclubs, bars, jobs, non-profit organizations, etc. Amazingly, the white LGBT community has managed to pull off a major finesse game using the very same Black people many of them victimize.

The white LGBT community branded themselves as an aggrieved "minority" group whose plight is comparable to Foundational Black Americans. White people in the LGBT community have never been enslaved, lynched, subjected to Jim Crow policies, or mass incarcerated. They knew it would be difficult to sell the idea that they are equally subjugated, so they came up with a strategy of pretending to ally with Black LGBT people. This phony partnership's main objective is not to share resources and benefits with Black LGBT people, but to use these Black people as mascots and Trojan horses to push social, legal, and political agendas that ultimately benefit the white LGBT community.

The white LGBT community will often run to the media with phony concerns like "Black Trans Lives Matter" and other empty slogans. They use the systematic disenfranchisement that all Black people suffer from, including Black gay people, to try to separate Black LGBT people from the rest of Black society. No one is oppressing white LGBT people. Therefore, they prop up disenfranchised Black people who happen to be gay or trans, and push for policies by using these Black people as mascots.

The white LGBT community uses gay Black people like white run NGOs used images of starving African children in the 1970s and 80s. Non-Governmental Organizations would produce television commercials showing images of starving African children from war-torn nations to ask people for money. The money to feed the poor, downtrodden children would go to the white people running these organizations, with few resources trickling down to the Africans presented in the propaganda images.

White LGBT organizations run the same hustle. They prop up images of gay Black people being harmed, usually in situations where systematic racial deprivation is the root cause of the situation. The white LGBT community will frame the harm as homophobic and then collect money for themselves, leaving the Black mascots holding an empty bag.

The Black and Brown Alliance Myth

One of the most common ally narratives pushed on Black society is the myth of the "Black and Brown coalition." Contrary to this propaganda, there has never been a Black and Brown alliance of any significant consequence between Black people and Hispanics. This alliance has always been one sided where Black people do all the fighting and groundwork to get tangible resources for "Brown" communities, while Black people get nothing in return.

Individual relationships between certain Black people and Hispanics have been harmonious. As a group, Black people have always been inclusive of Hispanics because we have always viewed them as an aggrieved minority just like us. As a group, Black people are the ones pushing the Black and Brown rhetoric.

While Black people and Black organizations were fighting for civil and equal rights that included Hispanics, prominent Hispanic organizations openly distanced themselves from

Black people and our struggle. In 1957, Felix Tijerina, the head of the oldest Hispanic advocacy organization in America, The League Of United Latin American Citizens, sternly stated: "Let the Negro fight his own battles. His problems are not mine. I don't want to ally with him" (Behnken, 2011).

This statement was indicative of the collective ideology of the Hispanic community then and now. Historically, Black people have assumed that Hispanics are fellow minorities and "people of color." Part of this assumption is because White Anglos will often practice certain levels of racism against Hispanics. Because we both share the same oppression, this leads Black people to falsely assume that Blacks and Hispanic share an ideological commitment to eradicating systematic white supremacy.

Black people assume, since white supremacists often view Blacks and Hispanics with racial contempt, that we have a natural commonality with Hispanics. The problem is, Foundational Black Americans and Hispanics don't view the white supremacists the same way. Most Hispanics identify with European culture. When it is politically beneficial, many Hispanics will claim to have some sort of indigenous heritage. But in places like Mexico, indigenous non-Spanish people are systematically discriminated against by the Hispanic population. The white identifying Hispanic masses view indigenous people as an ethnic "other."

Many people in the Hispanic community classify themselves as *white*. Even though they have often been subjected to systemic racism, they still see themselves as Europeans. Many people from Latin American countries who come to the

United States classify themselves as white instead of Indian or Native.

A common saying in Latin American countries is "Mejorar La Raza" meaning "improve the race." In essence, this means whiten up as much as you can in order to escape the Black bloodlines rooted in Latin America. Afro-Latinos in these countries are often marginalized and treated with contempt by white Latinos. When white Latinos immigrate to the United States, or anchor their children here, many bring that same anti-Black contempt with them as a group.

Interestingly, many Hispanics who come to the United States and classify themselves as white often go out of their way to deny this fact. When it's politically convenient, many of these Hispanics will identify as "people of color" to receive some form of tangible benefits, but ultimately they view themselves as white.

In places like Puerto Rico, where the African bloodline is still heavily present, over 75% of people still classify themselves as white. In Cuba, over 65% of people living there classify themselves as white.

In 1930 when the U.S. Census classified "Mexican American" as a distinct race, leaders of the Mexican-American community protested vehemently and had the classification removed from the very next census. The League of United Latin American Citizens complained that declassifying Mexicans as white was an attempt to "discriminate between the Mexicans themselves and other members of the white race, when in truth and fact we are not only a part and parcel but as well the sum and substance of the white race" (Gracias, 1989; Haney-Lopez, 2006).

Tracing their ancestry in part to the Spanish who conquered South and Central America, they regard themselves as off-shoots of white Europeans and not the indigenous people of the Americas. Many people are aware that many indigenous people in Mexico and the rest of the Americas, for that matter, were Black skinned people who would be classified as Black today.

In 1920, the enoted Hispanic historian Carlos Cuervo Marquez wrote in his book, *Estudios Arqueológicos y Etnográficos Americanos*, Vol. 1, that, "The Negro type is seen in the most ancient Mexican sculptures. It is likely that, we repeat, America was a Negro Continent."

Every Latin American country is rooted in African and/or Black indigenous ancestry and culture. Over a period of time, the Spanish speaking inhabitants of these lands tried to erase or ignore the Black part of their history and lineage. The carrot of honorary whiteness, which is dangled in front of Hispanics by the more Anglo white supremacists, has proved to be too good of a lure.

In countries where non-white people outnumber the white population, white supremacists learned how to create color castes to divide people with more pronounced African ancestry. Certain benefits and opportunities were allotted to people in these countries based on how close their physical characteristics were to Anglo European phenotypes. Systematic mistreatment and deprivation were reserved for people closer to the African phenotype.

In Argentina, which is considered the whitest of all the Latin American countries, the government committed a quiet genocide against the Black population in order to ethnically cleanse the nation. In the late 1700s, the majority of Argentina's population was Black. In the mid-1800s, Argentina's president Domingo Faustino Sarmiento instituted draconian policies to eradicate the Black population (Helg, 1990; Romero, 2021).

First, he segregated the Black population and deprived them of healthcare and resources, so they were reduced to living in squalor. Then he mandated the forced recruitment of the Black men into the military so they would be the first ones wiped out during the wars. These policies, as well as mass imprisonment for minor or fabricated crimes, and mass executions, ultimately led to the severe ethnic cleansing of most of the Black population of Argentina.

The country's racial cleansing tactics were so enticing to white supremacists that several thousand Nazis fled to Argentina after World War II. Even though Argentina's most popular cultural export -the tango dance- was created by Black Argentines (Collier, 2002; Karush, 2012), its Black people were tragically exploited. The free labor of the Black population was exploited to enrich Argentina, while Black people's culture was stolen and appropriated by white Hispanic Argentines, and the Black population was essentially wiped out.

The reality is that Foundational Black Americans in the grassroots and political arena have been the only people collectively pushing the one-sided Black and Brown myth. Foundational Black Americans are the ones pushing for immigration programs and protections that benefit the Hispanic community, while we get absolutely nothing tangible in return.

The only perceived "benefit" Black people get out of upholding the Black and Brown alliance myth is the potential to gain sexual access to Hispanic people. This is especially true for many Black men. The thought of getting exotic sex from Hispanic women unfortunately causes a lot of brothers to forfeit any strategies for getting tangible benefits for Black society.

Not only do we not get any benefits from this one-sided coalition, Foundational Black Americans are often systematically targeted with violence by white Hispanic police, civilians, and gangs. Black people are unjustly killed by white Hispanics like officer Jeronimo Yanez, who was protected by white supremacist society after he killed Philando Castile, an innocent Black man in Minnesota.

White Hispanic George Zimmerman was also protected by white supremacist society after he killed Trayvon Martin, an innocent child walking home from a store in Florida. None of the major Hispanic organizations spoke out against Zimmerman, Yanez, or any other case where white Hispanic officers or vigilantes committed unjust acts of violence against Foundational Black Americans.

Many Hispanic street gangs, especially in California, align themselves with white supremacist Skinheads and Aryan Nation groups if they go to prison. In Los Angeles, there are also many white Hispanics working in law enforcement who join white supremacist police gangs. Anti-Black sheriff's deputy gangs like the Spartans, Regulators, Grim Reapers, Banditos, and Executioners have operated within the ranks of law enforcement in Southern California for decades, to which the federal government turns a blind eye.

The point is that the Hispanic community, as a group, has always looked out for their best self-interests, and they continue to do so. There are individuals, and certain demographics within the Hispanic community, who are cordial and hospitable towards Foundational Black American society. But when it comes to empowering themselves as a group, Hispanics generally stay on-code with each other when it comes to dealing collectively with Foundational Black Americans. They are not in the business of sharing resources and power with Foundational Black Americans, and FBA should adopt the same ideological approach.

The Real Relationship Between Foundational Black Americans and Red Native Americans

The respected historian Carter G. Woodson famously stated:

"One of the longest unwritten chapters in the history of the United States is that treating of the relations of the Negroes and the Indians." (Brazelton, 2021; Teutsch, 2014)

Woodson was absolutely correct. The history of the relationship between Black people and Red Native Americans is something that white supremacists have gone out of their way to suppress. We have been told that white explorers came to the Americas starting in 1492, interacted with Mongoloid looking Native Americans, and Black people were only brought to North America in 1619.

This false narrative has been promoted heavily because the dominant society made it an imperative to hide the real history of Black people in America and our true relationship with Native Americans. Many Black people in the United States *are* Native Americans. Out of all the Black people in Africa who were captured and forced into the Trans-Atlantic Slave Trade, only 6% of those captives were brought to North America. Most were taken to the Caribbean, Central America and South America.

When European explorers arrived in the Americas, many documented their interactions with the Black aboriginal people already inhabiting the land. The reason Christopher Columbus called the natives he encountered "Indians" was because they resembled the Black skinned people of India.

The explorer Giovanni da Verrazzano famously documented when he arrived in North America that the natives he encountered in 1524 were "black in color, not unlike the Ethiopians, with thick black hair" (Borelli, 2020; Gerald, 2013). During that period, Ethiopian was a term used to describe all Black Africans.

In 1513, Vasco Núñez de Balboa met members of a "tribe of Ethiopians" in Panama (Forbes,1993). Several other European explorers made similar claims about interacting with Black aboriginal peoples. Centuries later in the 1800s, the noted white biologist Constantine Samuel Rafinesque was considered controversial by his contemporaries because he admitted that the Americas were populated by Black indigenous peoples at the time of European contact (Warren, 2014). Years later, other respected Black historians like Ivan Van Sertima released books like *They Came Before Columbus*, which documented all the powerful evidence of the Black aboriginal presence in the Americas.

This part of our history has been rigidly suppressed from consciousness. In order to psychologically control Foundational Black Americans, the dominant society must make us appear to be foreigners in our own land. By referring to us as African Americans, the dominant society reduces Black people to just another immigrant group that migrated to America from another country.

Foundational Black Americans are the only non-immigrant group in this country. We are descended from the enslaved Black people who were brought to the Americas starting in the 1500s. We are also descended from the Black aboriginal natives who lived in the Americas thousands of years before European contact. On top of having this unique lineage, Foundational Black Americans built the United States of America from the ground up. We did not immigrate to the United States, because there was no United States until Foundational Black Americans built it. We are literally the foundation of this nation.

When different European explorers tried to set up colonies in North America without the assistance of Black people, they all failed. In 1526 when the Spanish explorer Lucas Vázquez de Ayllón tried to establish the San Miguel de Gualdape colony in the current South Carolina/Georgia area, it failed. Ayllón brought 100 enslaved Black people with him to the colony. The enslaved Black people staged an uprising against the Spanish colonizers/enslavers that ultimately caused them to retreat (Matibag, 2003; Stone, 2021) back to their ships and flee towards the Caribbean. The Black rebels blended into the aboriginal native population.

In subsequent years, some Black aboriginal tribes like the Yamasee and others who battled against the European colonizers, ultimately lost these battles and ended up being enslaved. Eventually the lines were blurred between the Black people who were brought to the Americas from Africa, and the aboriginal Black people who were already on the land for thousands of years.

In many documents produced by the European colonizers, they often referred to the aboriginal people of the Americas as "negroes." Laws like the 1682 Virginia Slave Act essentially made terms like negro and Indian practically interchangeable (Evans Jr, 1962; Higginbotham, 1978). The law reads:

> "It is enacted that all servants [...] which shall be imported into this country... whether Negroes, Moors, mulattoes or Indians who and whose parentage and native countries are not Christian at the time of their first purchase by some Christian

[...] are hereby adjudged, deemed and taken to be slaves to all intents and purposes."

Eventually, the white supremacist Europeans would use divide and conquer tactics to better control the Mongoloid Natives and the Black aboriginal people who were mixed with Africans. The New York Treaty of 1790 allowed the Creek Indians to capture and return runaway slaves, particularly the Black Seminoles (Braund, 1991; Wright, 1967).

here were thousands of Aboriginal American tribes in the Americas before the arrival of Europeans. But in later years, the Europeans would designate only five of those tribes as "civilized." This term was broadly applied to the Creek, Choctaw, Cherokee, Chickasaw, and Seminole Indians because these particular Mongoloid looking tribes established economic ties with the white supremacists. These five tribes also participated in the enslavement of Black people.

It must be noted that the situation between Black people and the Seminoles was different from the other four so-called civilized tribes. Many Seminoles were Black runaway slaves and they were initially allies with the Red Seminoles against the white supremacists. Even the word Seminole is a variation of the Spanish word *cimarron*, which means runaway.

Seminole enslavement of Black people was often like a form of Feudalism. The Red Seminoles would often "own" Black Seminoles so that random white people could not claim ownership over them. The Black Seminoles were allowed to cohabitate in their separate communities. Black Seminoles were required to pay tribute to the Red Seminole leaders by providing a certain percentage of their yearly harvest.

While the native aboriginal ancestry of Foundational Black Americans was being erased, white supremacists started co-opting the lineage of Aboriginal Americans. In the late 1800s there was an Indian census called The Dawes Rolls. When the public found out that the Dawes Rolls would be used to give land allotments to members and descendants of the so-called Five Civilized Tribes, many white people showed up to be listed. Many of these whites would pay $5 under the table to a Dawes Rolls worker to list them as Indian (Debo, 1973; Otis, 2014). These people came to be known as $5 Indians - meaning phony Native Americans.

Many pale skinned people who claim Native American ancestry today are not even Native. Many of them are white people who finessed their way into a Native American identity or are descended from white people who did the finessing. Many of these PRETENDians descend from the white people who paid $5 to get on the Dawes Rolls. Other white people claim they were "adopted" by an Indian tribe, and are therefore entitled to the tangible benefits allotted to that tribe. The PRETENDian scam is fairly common in white supremacist circles. Reality TV personality Dog the Bounty Hunter, who was caught on tape delivering a vile anti-Black rant and who was also convicted of murdering a Black man with other accomplices in the 1970s, claims to be part Native American. Chapman claims to be of Cherokee descent, but many people have questioned the validity of that claim because both his parents are descended from European immigrants.

One of the most famous "Native Americans" from the mid-20th Century was an actor named Iron Eyes Cody. Cody portrayed Indians in many Hollywood films. In the early 70s he gained further notoriety by appearing in a PSA commercial about pollution, where he shed a single tear at the end of the segment. He became known as the "Crying Indian" because of that commercial.

For the remainder of his life, Iron Eyes Cody represented himself on and off camera as Indian. After his death, it was revealed that Iron Eyes Cody wasn't Native American at all. His real name was Espera Oscar de Corti and both of his parents were Italian immigrants. There was absolutely nothing "Indian" about Iron Eyes Cody or his lineage.

While white supremacists were falsely claiming Native American heritage, the authentic aboriginal heritage of Foundational Black Americans was being systematically erased. Starting in 1912, a white supremacist named Walter Plecker became the registrar of Virginia's Bureau of Vital Statistics. Plecker used his position to reclassify thousands of Native Americans who had Black features or any suspicion of Black ancestry as "negro" (Coleman, 2007; Scales, 2001).

Plecker was one of the people who popularized the "one drop rule", meaning that if a person was found to have one drop of Black blood in their ancestry, they would be classified as negro. The "one drop rule" prevented any tangible resources allotted to Indians and whites from trickling down into Black society.

As white $5 Indians began to infiltrate Indian tribes, they began to develop policies to kick Black Native Americans out of these tribes. Even though the Treaty of 1866 specified that Black Freedmen who were associated with the five civilized tribes were supposed to receive the same tangible benefits as the rest of the tribes (Foreman, 1989; Zissu, 2014), that part of the treaty was simply ignored. These exclusionary policies are still used against Black people today.

The Myth of Pan-Africanism

Debunking the myth of Pan-Africanism is a very touchy subject in Black society. For centuries, Foundational Black Americans have had our collective memories erased. The history of the indigenous Black American lineage has been hidden from us. We are taught the narrative that our only lineage comes from some far off, unknown country in Africa, centuries ago.

Black Americans are taught that we are visitors on this land, when in reality Black people have been in the Americas longer than any group, including the Mongoloid Red Indians. For centuries scholars have presented evidence that America was populated by Black aboriginals with so-called "Negroid features" for thousands of years. Yet the narrative that keeps being reiterated is that the only reason Black people are in the United States is because we were brought over on slave ships from Africa. As I stated before, this narrative is promoted to make Black people comparable to the other immigrants who came to the United States after the country was established. Foundational Black Americans are the only non-immigrant group in the United States. The Red Indians who had darker pigmentation have been absorbed into Black society, while the other Red Indians have been coopted into white society.

The reality is, Foundational Black Americans have two deeply rooted lineages. Our direct African lineage goes back at least 500 years, while our indigenous Black American lineage goes back thousands of years. When white supremacists started to enslave the Black aboriginals and Africans, they worked to erase the ancestral memories of both groups to better control and dominate Foundational Black Americans. This strategy has worked like a charm for centuries.

While other groups of immigrants who come to this land are told by the white supremacists who are currently in power that this land is now their land, Foundational Black Americans are made to feel that we are unwanted guests who have overstayed our welcome. Despite our presence on North American soil for centuries, and us literally building up the United States from scratch, we are told our real home is some random African nation that no longer exists.

The African side of Foundational Black American's lineage is descended from countries in Africa that have disappeared, fallen, been absorbed into other nations, or completely colonized culturally. Even though Foundational Black Americans have the same DNA and genetics as Africans in the diaspora, because of our unique experiences, migratory patterns, and enslavement, we are *culturally* distinct in many ways. Many Africans in the diaspora are aware of this.

The issue with Foundational Black Americans, is that we don't often realize that some Africans and Caribbeans see us as a different tribe. Foundational Black Americans look at all Black people as our brothers and sisters in the struggle against white supremacy, which is why Foundational Black Americans have pushed the Pan-African agenda for so long.

After slavery and during the Jim Crow era in America, Foundational Black Americans embraced the few African and Caribbean immigrants who were allowed to come to the States. It was Foundational Black Americans who pushed Jamaican immigrant Marcus Garvey into international prominence. In fact, Marcus Garvey repeatedly failed to get his vision of Pan-Africanism off the ground in the Caribbean. Even though today Marcus Garvey is promoted in Jamaica as a national hero, during his lifetime the Jamaican population simply wasn't interested in Garvey's ideas.

When Garvey moved back to Jamaica after his movement was sabotaged by the FBI in the United States, he ran for political office in his home country and lost to a white man named George Seymour-Jones (Cronon, 1960; Patsides, 2005). Garvey became so disenchanted with the people of Jamaica that he moved to Britain and vowed to never come back (Grant, 2008; Pereira, 2014). This points to the fact that Pan-Africanism was never really embraced by the Caribbean community as a whole.

In the United States, other Foundational Black Americans promoted the ideology of Pan-Africanism before Marcus Garvey. In the 1800s, Foundational Black Americans like Martin Delaney and Alexander Crummel discussed the importance of Black Americans, Caribbeans and Africans acknowledging their racial commonality in order to combat global white supremacy.

The Pan-Africanism ideology has never been largely reciprocated in other African and Caribbean cultures. In fact, there have always been opportunists from the diaspora who tried to capitalize off the ancestral confusion that many Black Americans have about their lineage. In the early 1900s, before Marcus Garvey's movement took off, there was another Back to Africa movement lead by a Gold Coast born immigrant merchant, Chief Alfred Sam.

Chief Sam came to the States and told Black Americans a bunch of tall tales about the wealth, resources and freedom available in Africa. He told people that where he was from in Africa, diamonds lay in the streets after it rained. He convinced hundreds of Black people to sell their possessions and "come home" to the Mother Land to escape the racism of America.

An initial group of 60 Foundational Black Americans arrived in West Africa with Sam. These settlers were discouraged by the conditions in Africa, and they felt misled by Sam's claims. To make matters worse, tribal leaders in the African countries would not allow Foundational Black Americans to own land.

The 500 or so other Black people in America who was waiting and ready for Chief Sam's ship to pick them up were abandoned, as he never appeared. Many Foundational Black

American families lost their life savings trying to invest in the one-sided dream of Pan-Africanism.

Even though people classified as Black are all treated the same by white supremacists globally, the issue is that all Black people globally don't have the same reaction to white supremacy. The strategies used to dominate Black people differ according to what part of the world they live in. Nonetheless, the same goal is reached - racial domination.

In Africa, white supremacists came from Europe and colonized the native people. Colonization is basically the same thing as slavery, and being dominated by systematic white supremacy is slavery. But because the word slavery wasn't used, the native Africans had an illusion of freedom. Deceptive words like "colonization" and "imperialism" were used to describe the white supremacist domination of Africa. These terms often gave African societies the idea that they were simply involved in a political struggle with the European powers.

The Europeans mastered the art of indirect domination of African societies by creating puppet leaders and putting them in positions of power. When the white supremacists orchestrate economic turmoil in African nations, the blame is usually levied at the Black puppet leaders. The white supremacists who orchestrated the turmoil and propped up the Black puppets in the first place are then viewed as saviors by many African people when they show up with "solutions" (i.e. food relief, medical supplies, etc.) for the problems they created.

Unfortunately, many African natives end up viewing white people as God-like saviors. Giant statues of white Jesus are all over Africa today. Many young Foundational Black Americans reject the image of a white Jesus Christ, even if they still subscribe to Christianity. This is further evidence that native Africans and Foundational Black Americans don't view whiteness with equal adoration. Therefore, our approaches for dealing with white supremacy often differ.

Black people in the Caribbean also have a different approach to white supremacy than Foundational Black Americans. In the West Indies during formal slavery, on these islands the white supremacists were often outnumbered by the Black population. To control the non-white masses, they had to create a multitude of different caste systems within Black society. They set up specific communities for different mixed race Black people and gave them certain privileges and benefits over unmixed Black people. This created competitive buffer classes on these islands. The privileged Black people (with names like creole, half-caste, free colored, mulatto, etc.) would fight to keep the unmixed Black masses from attacking the white supremacists in charge. The buffer class Blacks knew that their slightly privileged conditions were contingent on the white supremacists remaining on top.

Although some of these racial categories were used for Foundational Black Americans, there was no buffer class community of privileged Black Americans elevated over other Black people. All Black people in America were treated the same by the white supremacists. And color caste meant nothing because lighter skinned Black people in America faced the same racism as dark skinned Black people. In fact, white supremacists have always been more hypersensitive about light skinned Black people because they sometimes have the ability to sneak Black genes into white society undetected.

These circumstances caused Foundational Black Americans to view all non-white people, especially Black people globally, as one big group who are all victimized by white supremacy. While this is a correct observation, these other groups are allowed to come to America, and are incentivized by the white supremacists to act as buffer groups between white and Foundational Black Americans. Unfortunately, many African and Caribbean Black people are propped up by white supremacists to undermine Foundational Black Americans.

When it comes to positions of perceived leadership or political office in America, white supremacists will scientifically elevate non-Foundational Black American immigrants to "represent" Black people. A lot of white-run social justice organizations heavily promoted in the white media, like Black Lives Matter, engage in this practice. That particular organization tries to prop up a group of Black women, who mostly come from immigrant backgrounds, as spokespersons for Black society. That organization takes in millions of dollars off the deaths of Black Americans, and then they pivot to bringing attention to LGBT issues and policies that primarily benefit white LGBT people.

White supremacists understand that many Black immigrants don't have direct ancestral and cultural connections with Foundational Black Americans. These Black people will be more willing to stay off-code with the Foundational Black American masses, and tow the line for white supremacy.

White supremacists also make it a point not to allow too many Foundational Black Americans access to the top branches of political power in America. For example, people like Eric Holder and the late Colin Powell, two Black people who were in high-ranking political positions, both come from Caribbean backgrounds. Many people in the Congressional Black Caucus are Caribbean and African immigrants. The Congressional Black Caucus is infamous for not doing anything to specifically help Foundational Black Americans. In fact, in the 50 year history of the Congressional Black Caucus, no one can point to a single policy or tangible thing that the organization has accomplished for Foundational Black Americans.

There is a reason why non-FBA people like Barack Obama and Kamala Harris were chosen for high positions in the White House. They have the appearance of Blackness, but culturally they have nothing to do with the lineage of Foundational Black Americans. Obama's lineage comes from Kenya and Europe. Vice President Kamala Harris's lineage comes from India and Jamaica. White supremacists understand that people are more inclined to help those who come from their lineage. They understand that if Foundational Black Americans occupy serious political positions, they might feel like they have an ancestral obligation to help other FBA. They also assume that it's easier for a non-FBA political figure to ignore the needs and concerns of Foundational Black Americans because there is no immediate ancestral camaraderie. So when a 1st or 2nd generation immigrant politician engages in the same policies of benign neglect against Black people that the white political establishment perpetuates, they are less likely to have a guilty conscience about it.

The Pan-African ideology is generally one sided: Foundational Black Americans do most of the work and fight for benefits to help the Black immigrant class, but these sentiments have not been reciprocated. Foundational Black Americans don't get land grants or other fast-tracked policies that allow Black Americans to have dual citizenship in Africa or the Caribbean. The excuse that many people in the diaspora give for why their countries have not welcomed Foundational Black Americans is that it's the corrupt government's fault.

The United States government, which is arguably the most powerful government in the world, did not allow Black immigrants into the United States in significant numbers until the mid-1960s. It was Foundational Black Americans who fought against the powerful U.S. government to amend immigration laws so that Black immigrants could come to America. Going back to the 1930s, Foundational Black Americans mobilized all over the country, against the wishes of the United States government, to volunteer to go to Africa and fight the Italian invasion of Ethiopia. Foundational Black Americans are constantly fighting the white supremacist policies and actions of those who run the U.S. government.

The reality is that there is not a significant collective effort by the grassroots population of many African and Caribbean societies to create a Pan-African union with Foundational Black Americans. Caribbeans have an organization called CARICOM, which is a collective of 20 Caribbean nations whose purpose is to promote economic integration and co-operation among its members, to ensure that the benefits of integration are equitably shared, and to coordinate foreign policy. Foundational Black Americans are not included in this union. Yet Caribbeans get all types of set asides and benefits that Foundational Black Americans fight for when they immigrate to America.

In Africa, there is an organization called the African Union, which is a collective of members from 55 different nations. Foundational Black Americans were never invited to be a part of the African Union's membership. But when African immigrants come to the United States, they get access to resources from "minority" and "diversity" set aside programs that Foundational Black Americans have sacrificed their livelihoods for.

There are individuals allies from many of these non-FBA groups and societies who have the uttermost respect for Foundational Black Americans, our culture, and our struggle.

But the brutal reality is, as a collective group, Foundational Black Americans do not have, and never have had, any true allies that did anything to assist us beyond symbolic and intangible gestures. Almost every interaction Foundational Black Americans have with other groups eventually takes an exploitive turn. These groups ultimately use the struggle, labor, mistreatment and sacrifices of Foundational Black Americans to secure tangibles for their own groups.

It is imperative that Foundational Black Americans utilize the same strategy of being on-code with our immediate ethnic group first so we can accumulate tangible resources.

Once we secure the power and resources to sustain our community, then we can then look into the idea of a global network.

CHAPTER EIGHT

The "I'm White And I Say So" Rule

I remember the day in the late 1970s when my mother took me to re-enroll in Leeds Elementary School in Leeds, Alabama. This school had been newly integrated a decade earlier. I was around seven at the time and I was a very hyperactive, outgoing kid. I was also a big fan of the *Jaws* movies that were popular in the late 70s.

While enrolling at the school, my mother and I had a private introductory meeting with my soon-to-be 2nd grade teacher, a white woman named Ms. Talley. The classroom was empty, so I quickly became bored sitting off to the side while my mother conversed with my teacher. I got up and went to the chalkboard and drew a huge picture of a shark. Then I drew a stickman figure of the teacher being eaten by the shark.

When the teacher saw this, she immediately turned to my mother and told her how unusual and problematic my behavior was, and that I should be recommended to a remedial learning program. Begrudgingly, my mother took me to get an "assessment" on the recommendation of Ms. Talley. I don't remember too much about the facility I went to for the assessment, but I do remember the other Black children there who were also labeled "remedial".

hile at this facility, I interacted with the children there. I couldn't tell if the staff members were teachers or doctors; it was an extremely weird environment. I was at this facility for a few hours and at the end of the day, the staff told my mother that my issue was hyperactivity. The staff prescribed the drug Ritalin.

My mother wasn't really feeling all these little strange diagnoses these people were throwing out. But, assuming they were professionals who knew what was in the best interests of children, she reluctantly continued. I ended up taking Ritalin for a short period of time and remember that it made me feel extremely high and lethargic all the time. I was generally a very active kid, but that Ritalin made me want to stay in the house and lay down all day.

This new behavior freaked my mother out because I wasn't the same kid anymore. She immediately stopped the Ritalin and told the school not to recommend any more remedial programs. She told them I was normal and there was nothing wrong with me, and that I was going to attend regular classes. To be placed in special classes or remedial programs, the parents have to sign off. She let them know she wasn't signing off on anything like that. I went back to regular school, took my regular classes, and turned out just fine. The reality was, I never needed those remedial classes or behavioral drugs in the first place.

Because white people are running everything on the planet, Black people often assume everything a white person tells them is correct and in their best interests. Nothing can be further from the truth. The main collective goal for those in the dominant society is to maintain the system of white supremacy. This ideology is enforced in every area of activity, even in the education of children.

I would later find out that starting in the 1970s it was a common tactic for white teachers to recommend special education and remedial classes for Black children. After the Civil Rights bills of the 1960s, it became illegal to openly discriminate against Black people and enforce segregation based on race. When schools were forced to to racially integrate in the 70s, white officials within the school system came up with this new strategy to separate white kids from Black kids. As many Black children as possible were funneled into special education classes. They could claim that the segregation was not based on race but on *learning ability*.

The criteria used to judge who was learning impaired was determined by one thing and one thing only: The "I'm white and I say so" rule. My life could have been dramatically altered all because of a false learning assessment given to my mother by my white 2nd grade teacher. Growing up in the Jim Crow South, my mother was intuitive enough to question the validity of the teacher's assessment. My mother and my grandmother grew up in an era where they knew that some white people could not be trusted. They knew the importance of using their own judgment when engaging with people in white society because their words cannot just be taken to be facts.

Unfortunately, many Black people are programmed to believe everything a white person tells them and take what white people tell them at face value. This happens for two main reasons. First, everyday we are psychologically programmed to think that white is right. And, secondly, because the "I'm white and I say so" (IWAISS) rule is frequently backed up by systematic white supremacist force.

The Origin of the IWAISS Rule

Generally, the IWAISS rule has been enforced ever since the white supremacists first left Spain to subjugate the New World. Their clear objective was to conquer and dominate everyone and every place they might encounter. The white supremacists realized that once they conquered the Black Moors, who had ruled over areas of Southern Europe for more than 700 years, everyone else on the planet would be a piece of cake.

When the Europeans landed in new lands, they immediately started to enforce the IWAISS rule by renaming every place, person and thing. When Christopher Columbus landed on the island originally referred to as Ayiti by the Taíno natives, he renamed it "La Isla Española" (The Spanish Island), later shortened to Hispaniola. The Europeans also renamed the aboriginal inhabitants of the New World "Indians." They told the native peoples that their homelands would be dominated and ruled by Europeans and that the natives had to accept it.

The natives of the New World, and eventually every other non-white population across the world, had to accept the orders of the white supremacists for one main reason: the white supremacists shared a collective codified mindset with other Europeans, an understanding that they would dominate all the non-white peoples and they had the military muscle to back up their words and orders.

Non-white groups are still dominated by white supremacists today because most non-white people don't understand the IWAISS rule. This is an unspoken rule that white supremacists won't generally admit to. An essential trick of white supremacists is to make their victims believe that any harm done to them was their own fault. White supremacists will never reveal to their victims that most of the negative things that non-white people collectively suffered were orchestrated directly or indirectly by the white supremacists.

Black people in the United States ultimately saw the IWAISS rule solidified and officially put into law with the 1857 Dred Scott court case decision. The Dred Scott case, also known as Dred Scott v. Sandford, was a decade-long fight for freedom by Dred Scott, an enslaved Foundational Black American. The case persisted through several courts and ultimately reached the U.S. Supreme

Court. In a landmark decision, Chief Justice Roger Taney ruled that the U.S. Constitution was not meant to extend American citizenship to Black people, regardless of whether they were enslaved or free. In other words, the rights and privileges that the Constitution confers upon American citizens did not apply to Black people.

This Supreme Court opinion contains some of the most vile, anti-Black ideologies imaginable. One passage reads:

> "They (Foundational Black Americans) had for more than a century before been regarded as beings of an inferior order, and altogether unfit to associate with the white race, either in social or political relations; and so far inferior, that they had no rights which the white man was bound to respect; and that the negro might justly and lawfully be reduced to slavery for his benefit."

Today white scholars and historians often claim that this was the worst ruling ever made by the Supreme Court. People in the dominant society don't consider this ruling to be bad because of the Supreme Court's views on Black people. They see it as bad because the words and ideologies were written down and placed into the historical record. That was a no-no. White supremacists figured out the best way to maintain systematic white supremacy was to acquit themselves of any wrongdoing and blame the Black victims of white supremacy for causing their own misery through their pathological actions. The Supreme Court's Taney ruling proves that systematic white supremacy and anti-Black racism is based simply on Black people *being born*. White supremacists have designated Blackness as the wrong color to be born with under the system of white supremacy.

The Dred Scott ruling's problem is you are not supposed to state the plight of Black people so plainly and directly. White people who practice white supremacy are supposed to understand this code without having to spell it out explicitly. One of the most infamous lines from the Dred Scott Decision states:

"(Black people) had no rights which the white man is bound to respect."

This is the law of IWAISS in a nutshell. Scholars and historians claim the Dred Scott ruling was overturned after the 13th and 14th Amendments to the Constitution were implemented because these Amendments granted Black people citizenship and equal protection under the law. This turned out to be meaningless because when it comes to protecting Black people, the laws of the Constitution simply aren't *enforced*. These Constitutional amendments were rarely enforced after they were approved and Constitutional protections for Black people are not equally enforced today.

The "I'm white and I say so" rule of white supremacy, however, is fully enforced. People in the dominant society practice a form of *common law* racism, meaning there are unwritten rules and codes that maintain systematic white supremacy. White supremacists could put a million laws on the books, but they will keep an unwritten and a publicly unspoken understanding with each other that they should remain on-code and not enforce any laws that would protect Black people and punish white people.

The common law of white supremacy is the secret to that system's power. People who practice and benefit from white supremacy globally learn the rules and codes of white supremacy through osmosis. These rules and codes are not written down anymore, so the people who practice white supremacy have plausible deniability. At one point, white supremacists adamantly wrote down the rules of white supremacy in books, newspaper articles and laws. After enough people in the dominant society got on the white supremacist code, they realized that white supremacy would be more effective if they stopped writing down their tactics. They could continue to practice the same anti-Black racism by using and sharing a codified understanding of their practices.

This is why Black people who are victims of this form of white supremacy are so frustrated and confused. Black people spend so much time and energy trying to prove racism to white people, who will often simply deny it exists, because it's not generally documented.

Infamous Modern Cases Where the IWAISS Law Was Invoked

The Travon Martin Killing

When people think of openly white supremacist policies and acts against Black people, they often refer to the Jim Crow era. Many white people do this because they understand that denying present day white supremacy helps to maintain it. Many Black people try to play the psychological game of denial as well, but they have to snap back to reality when they may potentially fall victim to direct forms of white supremacy.

he 2012 murder of the innocent Black 17-year-old student Trayvon Martin and the subsequent acquittal of the white Hispanic perpetrator who killed him, George Zimmerman, provided many Black people with a collective wake up call.

Martin was walking home from the store when Zimmerman spotted him, and called 911 to report the child looked suspicious. Against the 911 dispatcher's instructions, Zimmerman, armed with a gun, invoked the IWAISS rule and began chasing the innocent teen. Zimmerman caught up with the victim and instigated an altercation. It is assumed that Trayvon Martin fought back to defend himself from being attacked by some man he didn't know, which is when Zimmerman shot and killed him. Police agencies, the white media, and whites in the judicial system all got on-code with each other, justified Zimmerman's brazen act, and acquitted him. The IWAISS rule was invoked and the dominant society got on-code by perpetuating the lie that Zimmerman was the victim and Trayvon the aggressor.

Many believed that the Trayvon Martin lynching and the codified support of his murder by the dominant society were in response to Obama's election. The optics of a Black man being in a high visibility position (notice I am NOT saying position of power - the reality is that Obama was a powerless

Black man who the white establishment placed in a tokenized position) was upsetting for many in the dominant
society. They needed some type of reassurance that white supremacy was still the law of the land.

The most assured way to make sure systematic white supremacy is still intact is to have a white person kill an innocent Black person and get away with it. When a suspected
white supremacist kills a Black person, it's imperative that
the Black person be *innocent*. A white person who murders a
Black person who is clearly guilty of some type of offense
will not elicit the same collective outrage from Black society
as an innocent Black person. This is why white society, including police, rarely kill Black people who are actually engaged in crime. Most of the Black people we see getting
murdered and lynched by race soldiers were usually minding
their own business when the white suspects instigated and
escalated an altercation.

Collective Black outrage over a white person killing a Black
person is very important to this process. White society uses
the outrage to display to Black people their systematic powerlessness because Black people generally won't be in a position where they can punish the white perpetrator. When
white supremacists lynched Black people during Jim Crow,
they not only took photographs of themselves next to the
dead bodies of the murdered Black victims, they also sent
these photos around the country as postcards.

Whites were comfortable carrying out these blatant murders
in public because they understood what the people who
wrote the Dred Scott ruling understood: In a system of white

supremacy, a Black person has no rights that the white man is bound to respect. This was and still is the common law of the land. Legal analysis claims that certain amendments to the Constitution nullified the Dred Scott decision, but when it comes to protecting Black people, the Constitution of the United States is ignored constantly. Lynchings during the Jim Crow era, as well as lynchings carried out by race soldiers today, are in clear violation of the 5th and 14th Amendments to the Constitution. These amendments clearly state that no one should be deprived of life without the due process of law. Black people are constantly murdered by race soldiers who use the arbitrary, IWAISS logic to justify their killings.

The 8th Amendment to the Constitution states that no cruel and unusual punishment should be inflicted on citizens. Yet Black people are regularly executed by race soldiers for the most minute and arbitrary reasons. The race soldiers are rarely punished for these racial executions.

The only rule that is consistently enforced in white supremacist society is the Dred Scott decision, which overrules the Constitution in all areas of activity.

The Mike Brown and Eric Garner Killings

These lynchings of Mike Brown and Eric Garner were significant for a number of reasons. Committed a month apart in July and August of 2014, these racial murders debunked the narrative that killings captured on video or with eyewitnesses would lead to justice. Black people were led to believe that if white society *saw* actual footage of a Black person being unjustly killed by police then white society would bring justice to the situation. As Black people sadly learned, witnesses and footage don't matter in a white supremacist society.

Mike Brown was killed when Brown, an 18-year-old Black teen, was walking home with a friend in Ferguson, Missouri. A white police officer, Darren Wilson, initiated an altercation with Brown after a dispatch call came in about some stolen cigars from a local store. Wilson ended up executing Mike Brown by shooting him multiple times.

After Brown was killed, the dominant society got on-code with several IWAISS lies to justify the killing. One narrative promoted by the white media claimed that Mike Brown brutally beat Wilson's face. When actual hospital photographs of Wilson's face were revealed after the killing, it was plain to see that there were barely any visible bruises. Some suggested that Wilson received no facial injuries at all.

Many Black eyewitnesses stated that they saw Mike Brown with his hands up before Darren Wilson killed him, but the authorities and white media essentially dismissed their narratives. The media ran with testimony from one of the white "witnesses" who appeared before the grand jury. A white woman, identified only as "witness 40," claimed that Michael Brown charged Darren Wilson "like a football player" before Brown was shot and killed. Many media outlets completely ignored the eyewitness testimony of the Black people and only ran the testimony of witness 40.

According to several reports that emerged after the grand jury decided not to prosecute Darren Wilson, the story told by witness 40's was apparently completely fabricated. Apparently witness 40 was nowhere near the crime scene when the murder happened. It was also reported by several media outlets that witness 40 was a racist who had a history of posting anti-Black rhetoric online (Holley, 2014; Marsden).

Even though transcripts indicate that witness 40's testimony wasn't taken seriously by the grand jury, her narrative still spread throughout the media. Witness 40 shows how white law enforcement, white media outlets, and white citizens all get on-code with each other to promote IWAISS narratives.

Eric Garner's murder was significant because it was one of the first incidents where the blatant, unjust murder of a Black person was caught on video and the killers went unpunished. Garner, a 43-year-old father of six, lived in Staten Island, New York. On July 17th, 2014 he was standing on a corner when he was approached by the police and ultimately choked to death by one of the officers. Contrary to many media reports, Garner was not selling cigarettes when the police approached him. Police asked Garner about selling cigarettes during previous encounters, but Garner was not in the act of selling cigarettes, nor was he committing a crime, when he was approached. The media deliberately ran the false narrative that Garner was selling loose cigarettes when he was attacked by police because the media's job is to provide the race soldiers with propaganda that will help to justify their racial terror. By falsely claiming Garner was selling cigarettes when the police officer approached him and choked him to death, this false premise establishes that Garner was in the process of committing a crime. If a Black person is said to be committing a crime, any punishment, no matter how severe, is justified under the system of white supremacy.

After Eric Garner was killed, many white media outlets doubled down on the IWAISS rhetoric, claiming Garner died not because a police officer choked him to death, but because he was overweight and had a heart attack. Essentially, they used the IWAISS defense to claim Eric Garner caused his own death. Conveniently, this claim means that Garner's Constitutional rights weren't violated and the sections that guarantee due process and equal protection under the law therefore didn't apply.

The Tamir Rice and Philando Castile Killings

One common point linking the killings of Tamir Rice and Philando Castile is that they were both committed in states with open carry gun laws. In 2014, Tamir Rice, a 12-year-old Black child, was in a park playing by himself with a toy gun in Cleveland, Ohio. A suspected white supremacist citizen called 911 on Tamir Rice, fully aware that he was a child. The caller even stated to the 911 dispatcher that Tamir Rice was "probably a juvenile" and that the toy gun "was probably fake."

The police arrived and immediately executed Tamir Rice in cold blood. The officers lied and tried to claim that they issued several commands that Tamir did not obey. However, surveillance footage of the murder clearly showed that the police opened fire within a couple seconds of arriving, executing Tamir.

After Tamir Rice's murder, the white authorities decided not to charge the officer who killed him. Using the IWAISS defense, they let the public know that what they saw with their own eyes was irrelevant. The white authorities said that Tamir was reaching for a weapon (what sense would it make for him to reach for a toy when the police pulled up?) and that the shooting was justified.

Ohio is an open carry state. If Tamir Rice had been an adult with a gun license (which an officer would not know until they carried out an investigation), it would not have been a crime for him to possess a gun. There was zero legal justification for the officer to immediately shoot Tamir Rice. If the officer knew Tamir was a child, it made no sense to shoot a child who posed no threat. If the officers thought Tamir was an adult, again, Tamir posed no threat and would have had a legal right to openly carry a gun. It would have been a potential violation of the 2nd Amendment to shoot and kill someone simply because they had a gun. This is why the IWAISS rule is so important to the white supremacists: they can tell people they saw what they didn't see. They can tell the public that a threat existed where there was clearly no threat. An entire system exists to support and spread these blatant lies.

The 2016 murder of 32-year-old Black man Philando Castile in Minnesota was another case that involved race and the 2nd Amendment. Castile was a passenger in a vehicle that was pulled over by a white Hispanic police officer, Jeronimo Yanez. When Yanez asked the female driver and Castile for identification, Castile calmly informed the officer that he had his weapon on him. Yanez immediately escalated the situation and shot Castile seven times, ultimately killing him.

Even though Castile was a legal gun owner, Minnesota is an open carry state, and Castile was completely innocent of any crime, a Minneapolis jury still acquitted Yanez for the murder of Castile. The 2nd Amendment did not apply to Castile. It was also revealed that two years before the killing, Officer Yanez attended a Bulletproof Warrior seminar, a controversial training program for law enforcement officers conducted by a retired Army Lieutenant Colonel named Dave Grossman (Rau, Buchanan et al., 2021). These courses teach trainees that, essentially, all police violence against citizens is justified. The Bulletproof Warrior training also teaches officers to shoot someone the second they feel threatened in any way (Hunt, 2021).

These courses teach officers that they are at war with the streets. This could be interpreted as a coded term for saying that cops are at war with Black society. Much of this Bulletproof Warrior training, for example, is not applied to white society or other groups but only to Black people. Some police agencies in certain cities don't allow their officers to participate in this training because its controversy would taint the public image of the department. The city of Minneapolis eventually banned the Warrior-style training of their police officers after uprisings against continued police brutality and violence in the city.

One of the unspoken (and sometimes spoken) perks of Warrior-style police training and membership for certain police unions (which often act as white supremacist protection rackets) is that they not only train and coach officers on how to kill people, but they provide them with the legal jargon and excuses they need to get away with it. These methods disproportionately target unarmed Black people, especially when the officer is white. When the officer is Black and the victim white, there is generally a different outcome.

When a Black Minneapolis police officer named Mohamed Noor shot and killed a white woman named Justine Damond, all the "Blue Wall" and "Back The Blue" talk went right out the window. Officer Noor was immediately prosecuted and sentenced to 12 years in prison.

The O.J. Simpson Trial

The 1995 murder trial of O.J. Simpson is one of the most infamous court cases in modern history. Its popularity and significance even decades after the verdict is due to the fact that it is one of the few cases involving a Black person where the "I'm white and I say so" tactic didn't work. Not only did it not work, the IWAISS tactic actually backfired.

The white media has twisted the narrative of this trial to make it seem like a guilty Black man was wrongfully acquitted for killing two innocent white people. This case had several elements that the white media knew they could play up in order to tantalize the public. First, O.J. Simpson was a famous Black man and that was an immediate draw. Second, the media knew they could play up the "Black Brute" stereotype, telegraphing the message that no matter how successful a Black man becomes, he should still be considered a threat due to his allegedly murderous nature. As we know, this particular stereotype is based much more on projection than reality.

This case was also captivating because it had the elements of the Othello narrative. In Shakespeare's classic play, the Black Moorish character Othello was married to a white woman named Desdemona. Othello ends up killing his white wife because he suspected her of infidelity. Tragic narratives like Othello have always been used by the dominant society as a cultural warning to white women about the fabricated dangers of entering into in a relationship with a Black man.

The first blockbuster Hollywood film, *The Birth of a Nation*, also played on this racist trope. This film featured a narrative of the Black male brute who so uncontrollably lusted after a white woman that she opted to kill herself rather than be savagely raped by the Black man (who was actually played in the film by a white man wearing Blackface). The "Black" man is later hunted down and lynched by the Ku Klux Klan.

This O.J. case had similar undertones. Commentary alleged that O.J. Simpson was an abusive Black brute who was jealous that his white wife had moved on from him. In his desire to have her back, he decided to kill her. Mark Fuhrman, a suspected white supremacist detective with the LAPD, came in to avenge the white woman's death, just like the Ku Klux Klan in the Birth of a Nation.

Another element that made the O.J. Simpson trial significant was that this case occurred in Los Angeles only a couple years after the 1992 LA Riots. In response to the beating of Black motorist Rodney King, a large scale rebellion erupted. The trial of the white officers who perpetrated the beating was strategically moved to a predominantly white suburb called Simi Valley. After the officers were acquitted, the City of Los Angeles exploded in a rebellion that lasted for days. When the smoke settled, there was over a billion dollars worth of damage, the reputation of the city was in shambles, and several white people were injured or killed.

The dominant society doesn't like to admit when it suffers a loss at the hands of Black people. Many people in the dominant society pretended to be unaffected by the LA Riots by repeating sentiments like "Blacks are destroying their own neighborhoods." The reality is, most businesses in Black areas, then as now, are owned by non-Black people. Another social data reporting trick the dominant society implemented was to manipulate racial death tolls after the LA Riots. They broke up the number of white deaths according to ethnic groups so that a white person from a hispanic background wasn't counted as a white death but a Latino death.

When it came to the number of Black people who died during the riots, officials grossly padded the numbers. They documented almost every Black person who died in and around Los Angeles during the week of the riots as a riot-related death. Many of those deaths had absolutely nothing to do with the riots. Black people who died in car accidents during the week of the rebellion were listed as riot-related deaths. White authorities attempted to save face and give the impression that Black people were affected more by the riots than white society was. But deep down, the white supremacists in charge understood the reality of what had happened.

So much property was destroyed and so many white people were killed and injured during the LA Rebellion that the white power structure wanted revenge on the Black citizens of Los Angeles. When the O.J. Simpson case entered the spotlight, they saw a perfect opportunity.

The authorities had a problem however: using the "I'm white and I say so" rule in the O.J. case would be tougher because they had just used it to acquit the white cops who abused Rodney King. The outcome was so devastating that the authorities knew they could not use the same deceptive tactics, back to back, in another high profile case. Dirty tricks like moving the trial to an all-white suburb wouldn't work – they had to have a *fair* trial. And that was the problem. In the system of white supremacy, there cannot be equal treatment between Black people and white supremacists. White supremacists must always possess an unfair advantage.

The O.J. Simpson trial was the most fair case in history, which is why so many people in the dominant society had a problem with the case. They viewed the fact that the IWAISS rule didn't work in this particular trial as a blow to systematic white supremacy. When O.J. Simpson was acquitted of double murder, many people in the dominant society were outraged because the white media put so much effort into portraying him as guilty.

The dominant society also viewed the O.J. verdict as a chink in the armor of systematic white supremacy because of the Black visuals that surrounded the case. The image of a Black man on trial being acquitted with the help of a Black lawyer, with a mostly Black jury deciding the case, with Black rebels in the street waiting in the wings to react to any judicial misconduct, was too much for many in the dominant society to process.

The white media played up the "guilt" angle in this case because it was more profitable. The "O.J. did it" narrative has become its own cottage industry that still generates money today. Many people have built careers directly and indirectly from that case. The Kardashian empire was thrust into the spotlight because the family patriarch, Robert Kardashian, was associated with O.J. Simpson during the trial. There have been countless book deals, movies, and television shows about the O.J. trial that have generated billions of dollars.

If a narrative of O.J.'s innocence was heavily promoted by the media, the story would have fizzled out the first week after the murders occurred. The reality is, when we seriously observe the O.J. Simpson case, it is clear that O.J. is innocent and had nothing to do with those crimes. When you look at the basic premise of the media narrative and the prosecution's explanation for and details about the murders, it actually sounds ridiculous. According to their narrative, on the night of June 12th, 1994, O.J. Simpson was getting ready to fly to Chicago for a planned appearance when he "snapped" and remembered how he abused his ex-wife who he had divorced two years before. For absolutely no reason, he decided to go to her house and kill her the same night he planned on taking a flight.

Continuing this narrative, O.J. Simpson put on a sweatsuit and some Bruno Magli dress shoes and headed over to his ex-wife's house armed with a knife. O.J. allegedly tried to "disguise" himself by wearing a skull cap and some small gloves that didn't fit (during the trial, one of the prosecuting lawyers, Christopher Darden, had O.J. try on the gloves found at the crime scene - it was proven on national television the gloves didn't fit). We are told to believe that O.J., wearing a skull cap, was somehow supposed to prevent his ex-wife from recognizing him when he "snuck up on her."

Never mind the fact that in America there is no history of a Black male millionaire ever committing murder. O.J. Simpson, according to the prosecution's bogus narrative, would be the first. But the narrative continues with O.J. going to the his ex-wife's house, where there is a dog barking incessantly at O.J. Never mind that O.J. bought the dog for Nicole and the dog was familiar with him. The skull cap disguise must have been too convincing for the dog.

They claimed O.J. Simpson creeped up on his ex-wife and stabbed her to death. O.J. was also able to stab Nicole Simpson's friend, Ron Goldman, who just happened to be there at the time of the attack. Never mind that Ron Goldman was younger and more fit than O.J., and that Ron Goldman was trained in martial arts. Medical investigators found several defensive wounds on Goldman's hands, showing that he violently fought back against his attackers. Yet when O.J. Simpson was physically examined after the murders, O.J. didn't have any scratches, wounds, or bruises on his face or body.

According to the prosecution, after O.J. committed these two murders with a knife, while wearing a ridiculous outfit and gloves that don't fit, he was able to dispose of the bloody clothes and knife, never to be found. O.J. was able to do all of this and get back home without any bruises to his body within a span of 25 minutes.

After the murders, a suspected white supremacist detective who had made a previous call to O.J. and Nicole's home a few years earlier went to O.J.'s house around 5:00 am. When Detective Mark Fuhrman realized O.J. wasn't at home, he decided to jump over the wall of the estate – without a warrant – and go to the back of O.J.'s house where he conveniently "found" a still-wet, bloody glove that didn't fit O.J. We are told to believe that O.J. masterfully got rid of the bloody clothes and the murder weapon, which are so well hidden that to this day they still haven't been discovered, but O.J. was also so dumb that he left a bloody glove right behind his house.

The media played up the prosecution's version of events everyday on the television news and in every other form of media. They buried any information that pointed to O.J. being innocent. One eyewitness, for example, a woman named Mary Ann Gerchas, was going to testify for the defense that she saw four suspicious looking men running away from the crime scene. But the prosecution, working with law enforcement, arrested Gerchas on "fraud" charges (Fisher, 1996) as a way to sully her image and credibility.

Anyone who came forward with information pointing to O.J.'s innocence would have been a problem not just for the prosecution, but also for the LAPD. If it was proved that O.J. was innocent, then that would also prove that the LAPD planted the evidence. According to the details of the evidence, and the testimony of Mark Fuhrman, it is likely that they did plant the evidence found at the crime scene and at O.J. Simpson's house. O.J.'s defense team unearthed an audio recording of Mark Fuhrman using the most vile, genocidal, and anti-Black rhetoric imaginable. In these recordings, Fuhrman admitted that he had planted evidence on innocent Black people. When Fuhrman was put on the stand during the trial, one of the defense lawyers asked him if he planted or manufactured evidence in the case. Instead of saying "no," as an innocent person would, Fuhrman plead the Fifth.

The media and the prosecution tried to portray Mark Fuhrman as some sort of "rogue" cop who did not represent the values and ideologies of the rest of the LAPD. In reality, Fuhrman represented everything the corrupt LAPD was about. Many people believe that Fuhrman was not working alone when he allegedly planted evidence.

LAPD Detective Philip Vannatter drew Simpson's blood at an LAPD station on June 13, the day after the killings. Instead of booking it into evidence, Vannatter put the vial with Simpson's blood in his pocket and went to Simpson's home where forensics was collecting evidence. So people are justified in their suspicions about this type of behavior.

The media also ignored other significant revelations related to the killings of Nicole Simpson and Ron Goldman, including the fact that some of their friends were killed in a similar manner around the same period. Nightclub owner Brett Cantor, who was friends with both Ron and Nicole, was killed in a similar manner (Dear, 2014). Cantor was stabbed, and the way his throat was cut suggested that the same people who killed him might have killed Ron and Nicole.

One of Ron Goldman's coworkers at Mezzaluna restaurant was also killed. Michael Nig, a waiter, was shot and killed in

Hollywood (Flowers, 2001), and it was a murder that was never solved. Allegations of criminal activity surrounding Mezzaluna Restaurant had been rumored for years. There were allegations that another employee at the restaurant barely escaped a car bomb (Campbell, 2015; Karyagdyyev, 2019). The media keeps quiet about this information whenever the O.J. Trial is discussed.

The O.J. Simpson trial had a fair, predominantly Black jury, as well as a leading Black defense lawyer, the legendary Johnnie Cochran, who brilliantly argued the case for O.J. And there were Black rebels in the streets ready to enforce justice. In this instance, the IWAISS rule could not be implemented in the court of law, but the dominant society made sure to use the IWAISS rule in the court of public opinion.

In an act of revenge years after the murder trial, the dominant society was able to use the IWAISS rule in court against O.J. In 2008, Simpson was sentenced to 33 years in prison for "stealing" his own items, the first time in American history that a person received such a sentence for stealing back their own stuff. O.J. was propositioned by one of his white associates to go and retrieve items that had been stolen from him. This white associate, however, was wearing a secret recording device and baited O.J. into going into a hotel room in Las Vegas, with some other men as backup, to retrieve some of O.J.'s memorabilia that was being sold by nefarious collectors.

The IWAISS rule was used to convict O.J. of robbery and kidnapping. On the secret audio recording, O.J. said, "don't let nobody out of here," in reference to the alleged thieves.

The court ruled that constituted "kidnapping." O.J. eventually served nine years of his sentence before he was paroled in 2017. His white associate, who set everything up, was granted complete immunity and received over $200,000 from selling the audio tapes to the media.

The Bill Cosby Case

The railroading of Bill Cosby is yet another example of the IWAISS rule at work. Cosby was convicted and sentenced to 3 to 10 years in prison for aggravated indecent assault of a white woman. There was zero evidence against Cosby and the white media repeated the lie that Cosby "confessed" to drugging women in a taped deposition. In the transcripts of the deposition, Cosby clearly denied giving women drugs without their knowledge. But that was ignored because the IWAISS common law, overrules any facts under the system of white supremacy.

The dominant white society understood there was no actual proof against Bill Cosby, so they claimed the "proof" was that a *number* of women made accusations against him. This is the epitome of the IWAISS rule. The majority of women making the allegations against Cosby were white, with a few non-white women sprinkled in that were mostly non-Foundational Black Americans who come from cultures that identify with whites.

This guilty-by-multiple-accusation tactic, without any tangible proof, only works against Black people. Large numbers of Black people accuse white supremacists and suspected white supremacists of crimes and violations all the time, but these accusations often get ignored even when there is actual proof. White people are rarely criminally punished based solely on the accusations of Black people.

In the Bill Cosby case, many of his accusers were proven to be liars. Many were represented by the same law firm that was trying to get Cosby to agree to a financial settlement. Many people believe the entire propaganda attack on Cosby was part of a money grab. One of the many Cosby accusers who the white media propped up was a woman named Shawn Upshaw Brown, whose daughter, Autumn Jackson, went to prison in the 90s for trying to extort $40 million from Cosby (Weiser, 1999; Westen, 2019).

It is my conjecture that if Bill Cosby was guilty of the accusations, there would be no need for the dominant white society to use deceptive tactics in the media and the court system in order to convict him. Several of the white female accusers claimed Cosby drugged and raped them, yet they claimed they repeatedly went back to Cosby to get re-drugged and re-raped again. The media propped up and co-signed this type of deception, which is an insult to women who really are sexually violated.

Many people compared these accusations to the Jim Crow era phenomenon of white women having consensual sexual relationships with Black men (and in many cases, no sexual contact at all) and then claiming they were raped.

The media and the lawyers involved in the case must have been aware of the visual associations of multiple white women making rape allegations against a Black man. Many people

accused the lawyers who were representing some of the accusers of "blackening up" some of the accusers with ethnic
backgrounds. Some of the more ethnic looking accusers
started to appear in the media with large afros and outdated
70s Blaxploitation looking outfits. The message that was being conveyed was that the railroading of Cosby isn't racial
because a few of these Black looking women were accusing
him as well.

The Importance of Racial Lies

A very important part of the culture of white supremacy is
the ability to make up arbitrary lies about Black people, and
then punish Black people based on those lies. This gives people in the dominant society a feeling of a God-like power
over the victims of white supremacy. Under the system of
white supremacy, Black people generally cannot punish white
people, no matter how unjust or heinous the infraction,
without the permission or approval of other white people.

Under the system of white supremacy, if a Black person tries
to punish a white person for any wrongdoing without the assistance or approval of other white people, then it's the Black
person who will most likely end up being punished. When
Black people try to stand up against the suspected race soldiers in law enforcement who commit racial ambush killings,
Black people are often punished or threatened with punishment by the dominant society. This is why white supremacist
society spends billions of dollars on militarized weapons and
enforcement to subjugate and threaten Black protesters
around the country.

Black people who defend themselves from white criminal suspects are often punished and jailed for standing their ground. The underlying message to Black people from the dominant society is to never take justice into your own hands against white people. Black people must find a white person to get justice for them.

Black people cannot make legitimate accusations against a white person that will result in punishment of the white person, and Black people definitely can't make false accusations against white people that would lead to punishment. Everything has to be filtered through, co-signed and approved by other white people. On the other hand, white people can make the most asinine accusations against Black people and accusations will result in punishment. White people can call the police on Black people, and falsely claim the Black person was threatening someone, and white race soldiers will immediately show up and oftentimes punish the Black person.

Historically, the system of white supremacy has granted white people permission to make up false rape allegations against Black people that have resulted in lynchings and other types of white supremacist violence. Key historical events in America that resulted in significant violence and rebellion were the result of false rape allegations against Black males by the dominant white society. The Tulsa Race "Riot" of 1921 and the 1923 Rosewood Massacre in Florida were both initiated due to false rape allegations made by white supremacists against Black males (Burke, 2020). Many historians believe the Civil Rights Movement of the 1950s and 60s, which led to a nationwide wave of violence and death in an effort to make social change, really kicked off after the gruesome murder of a 14-year-old Black child named Emmett Till, who was accused of making a sexual pass at a white woman in Mississippi.

A culture of directing IWAISS lies against Black people is used extensively in the present day, especially in interactions with law enforcement. Race soldiers within law enforcement have been given a common law green light to murder Black people, and they use the most ridiculous lies to justify their violence. Lies such as "I feared for my life" and "I thought he had a weapon" instruct the dominant society to get on-code with each other to support these lies. White supremacists would also get on-code with each other during Jim Crow in order to protect people in their community who lynched Black people.

These lynchings were often photographed and no one involved was ever prosecuted. White supremacists have one of the most rigid "no snitching" codes in modern history. All the people who benefit from the system of white supremacy are never supposed to snitch on one another when it comes to harming Black people. If a white person exposes a suspected white supremacist who harmed a Black person, generally the white whistleblower will often be labeled a nigger lover. Consequently, white society will often ostracize a white person who wants to do the right thing by producing justice for Black people.

CHAPTER NINE

Common Deception Tactics of White Supremacy

In the year 2000, I released my first bestselling book, *The Art of Mackin'*, a hugely popular book about dating and relationships that was meant to be a counter to all the *Men Are From Mars* relationship books that were popular at the time. I wanted to write a book that reflected how people really viewed the dating scene. Many dating books at the time were written by doctors and psychologists, and some of their advice came across as a little corny in my opinion. I wrote a book on dating from the perspective of a young dude who was out in the dating scene. I used a lot of the language and terms that all demographics could generally relate to.

The book was, and still is, a huge seller. *The Art of Mackin'* also kicked off the "pick up artist" wave that became popular in the early and mid-2000s. The book generated a lot of publicity and the *New York Times* gave the book a very positive review. I started to appear on many national radio and television shows to discuss the book. Initially, television producers thought they were going to bring me on these shows in order to disparage me and the book because it was a pretty bold move to come out with a book that unapologetically taught men how to have a player mentality when navigating the dating scene. Many radio and television producers thought they were going to have a field day picking apart the book.

By this point in my life, I understood how deceptive people in the dominant society could be, so I was always prepared when I appeared on certain programs. One television show in particular tried to use deceptive tactics but I was prepared for it.

When the *Art Of Mackin'* was initially released, one of the first nationally syndicated television shows that contacted me was the *Jenny Jones Show.* The show's producers contacted me and said they wanted to do an episode on guys who needed "mack make-overs." They told me they were going to get guys who thought they were players to come on the show and I was supposed to give them expert advice on how to step up their game.

Keep in mind, the *Jenny Jones Show* had a reputation for doing bait-and-switch ambush shows. They would contact guest and tell them they would be on the show for one topic, and then during the actual taping blindside them with another topic. There was an infamous murder case associated with the *Jenny Jones Show* because of their bait and switch tactics. In 1995, the show's producers contacted a man named Jonathan Schmitz and told him he had a secret crush, and that they wanted to reveal it on the show. Schmitz later stated that the producers implied that the crush was a woman and that's why he agreed to appear on the broadcast. When Schmitz appeared on the show in front of a live studio audience, the crush was revealed to be his gay male neighbor Scott Amedure. After the taping, Schmitz was allegedly so embarrassed by the encounter that he shot and killed Amedure. The Amedure family sued the *Jenny Jones Show* in a wrongful death lawsuit because of their ambush tactics.

When the producers of the *Jenny Jones Show* reached out to me, I knew it would be a great opportunity to promote my new book. I was also instinctively suspicious that they would try to pull a bait-and-switch. The theme of the episode was going to be called "From Wack To Mack" or something corny like that. I already knew these white producers were going to try to play on outdated 70s stereotypes. I remember one of the producers kept asking me to wear distinct clothes and to be sure to wear a large "mack hat" if I had one. I played right along and told them I would wear all that stuff.

I flew out to Chicago on the day of the taping and I waited backstage, preparing to go on. I was in one of my normal, relatively conservative playa suits. Nothing too flashy or gaudy. One of the producers come up to me and asked, "Hey Tariq, where is your hat?" I told him I was going to put it on right before going onstage, knowing that I had no hat and no intention of wearing one.

The other guests who were about to go on were wearing these goofy, stereotypical "mack" outfits, hats and all. I knew the purpose of the whole show was a set up to make a buffoonish presentation, filtered through the eyes of white people, of what macks and players are supposed to look and act like.

As the taping began, several men were paraded onstage wearing their goofy outfits while babbling about how mackish they were. Jenny Jones and the studio audience had a field day roasting these guys onstage. I had initially been told that I was going to be one of the judges for all these guys being brought out onstage, but I realized when my turn came that the segment was going to focus on me.

Jenny Jones introduced me and announced the title of my book, *The Art of Mackin'*, and showed the book's cover. As she introduced me, she had a sarcastic look on her face that essentially said "this guy had the nerve to write a book on how to be a player." The audience is showing me love as I come on stage and sit down. Immediately Jenny Jones starts grilling me about writing a book teaching men how to manipulate women, or something to that effect. I think she expected me to start bragging about how big of a player I was and how great I was with the ladies, but I took all the focus off me and started to break down the game. I told Jenny Jones and her audience, "We have to clear up some basic definitions and understand the difference between players, pimps, and macks. Players are sexually motivated. Pimps are financially motivated. And macks are motivated by learning game. Once a mack learns the game, you get sex and money at your disposal."

When I said that, the audience erupted into applause. They were eating the game up. Jenny Jones seemed to be thrown off by this. She didn't expect the audience to actually be on my side. She tried to grill me some more but I kept the focus off myself and remained focused on dropping general game. After that broadcast, *The Art of Mackin'* started flying off shelves around the country.

The lesson I learned from the Jenny Jones experience is that Black people must always be aware of the dominant society's deception tactics. We have to always be cognizant of any and all manipulative practices so that we can side-step the traps and pitfalls set up against us. When we recognize and understand these tactics, not only can we avoid their negative effects, we can actually turn the situations to our advantage.

For example, the *Jenny Jones Show* producers tried to get me on the show to promote outdated (and borderline racist) stereotypes of players and macks. They were planning on demonizing me in the process, but I played past their manipulation and took control of the narrative. I promoted myself and my book in my own words, and the *Art of Mackin'* started selling like hotcakes immediately after the episode aired.

Black people must fully understand that when you interact with people from the dominant society, there is a high possibility that deception may come into play. The legendary book, *The Art of War* by Sun Tzu, states that all warfare is based on deception. White supremacy is warfare and its greatest strength in the anti-Black war is deception. This is why it is crucial to recognize all forms of deception from white supremacist society.

There are seven general deception tactics that white supremacists and suspected racists use when they interact or engage with Black people.

1. Temporary Denial of Whiteness

When a suspected white supremacist is confronted or called out for an allegedly racist deed, the white person will often pretend to be naïve. They will often go into full deception mode. White supremacy is something that the dominant society does not want to seriously or logically discuss at length because any intelligent discussion about systematic white supremacy will expose its fallacies. At some point, the conversation will veer into discussions on what to *do* about systematic white supremacy. And many people in the dominant society do not want to get into discussions about taking actionable measures to dismantle the system of racism because they want to *maintain* the system.

Before the 1970s, white supremacists would proudly admit their white supremacist views. They wore their white supremacist ideologies as a badge of honor. But they eventually realized that boldly practicing white supremacy would generate bold opposition to these practices. We saw this bold opposition in the 1960s during the multiple racial rebellions that erupted around the United States. White supremacists had to refine their approach, and the new refined form of white supremacy is *denial*. No matter how much evidence is presented, white supremacists must deny the existence of systematic white supremacy at all costs.

When a person classified as white is suspected of supporting, defending or practicing white supremacy, often they will also temporarily deny their whiteness   in a desperate attempt to shield themselves from being labeled as racists. They will deceptively try to focus on some ethnic or religious heritage. A suspected white supremacist might try to claim they can't be a white supremacist because they are Hispanic, Jewish, 1/6th Native American, and so on. Many of these ethnic and religious identities that these suspected white supremacists try to claim can still be classified as white. The suspected white supremacists are fully aware of this.

Their objective is to deflect away from the topic of white supremacy by any means. The best way to deny being a beneficiary of white supremacy is to deny being white. Once these people get around other people classified as white, they will go back to claiming their white classification and will continue to take advantage of the privileges and benefits that go along with being classified as white.

2. Using Cherry Picked Stats

A common trope used by white supremacists in America today is "Black people are 13% of the population, but commit 50% of the homicides." There are several different variations of this phrase. White supremacists go on and on pulling out bogus stats about Black people committing crimes. This is an 'I'm white and I say so" tactic that is used to justify white society systematically harming Black people. The problem with bogus crime stats is that many low self-esteem Black people are deceived into regurgitating these misleading stats. Other non-white buffer groups will also start to cite these stats against Black people.

Black people do not commit crime at higher rates than other groups. The reality is that Blacks are *criminalized* much more aggressively than other groups. That's a major difference. Black crime stats have always been high in America because more things are illegal for Black people. During Jim Crow, Black people were arrested and prosecuted for walking on the wrong side of the street, entering the wrong racially designated doors, drinking from the wrong water fountain, etc. White supremacists would openly criminalize Black people for violating racially based policies.

The same phenomenon exists today, but the white supremacists use coded language in order to hide their racial intent. Using the "I'm white and I say so" rule, white supremacists will claim that Black people deserve to be systematically criminalized, harmed or murdered by members of white society for arbitrary reasons. Today, Black people are criminalized for things that other groups are simply not targeted for. Black people are the only group that is consistently criminalized (and in many cases, legally murdered) for driving in the wrong (i.e. white) neighborhoods, "looking suspicious", "resisting arrest", and other types of "I'm white and I say so" accusations. Bogus crime stats are used to justify the perpetual targeting of Black people and it is important that Black people do not internalize the deceptive propaganda behind these stats.

For over a century, bogus crime statistics have been used to project a culture of criminality onto Black society in order to justify harming and depriving Black people of resources. In 1896, the white supremacist Frederick Ludwig Hoffman wrote a book called *Race Traits And Tendencies of the American Negro*. Analyzing hospital records, mortality rates and criminal statistics, this book concluded that Black people had a natural propensity for criminality. By claiming that these findings were based on statistics and data, white supremacists like Hoffman and others could try to deny any personal racist predispositions.

Frederick Ludwig Hoffman ultimately became president of the American Statistical Association, and a statistician for a major insurance company. Hoffman used his statistics to claim that Black people were more disease prone, which was used by insurance companies to justify charging Black people higher premiums (Lawrie, 2013; Wolff, 2006).

Fast forward to the current era. The NFL recently underwent a scandal where payouts from a billion dollar brain injury settlement were distributed in a racially discriminatory manner. The NFL insisted on using a scoring algorithm for dementia testing that assumed that Black men started with lower cognitive skills. Therefore they would have to score much lower than whites to demonstrate sufficient mental decline to qualify for a financial settlement. The practice, which went unnoticed until recently, made it harder for Black former players to secure awards. The tactic of using statistics anchored in scientific racism has not changed.

3. Gaslighting

White supremacists enjoy the benefits and privileges they receive from the system of white supremacy. Acknowledging that this unjust system benefits them and that it exists would mean that they would have to take responsibility and do something to dismantle the system. In order to maintain the system they benefit from, white supremacists must project their bigotry onto the victims of white supremacy. While they do this, they engage in oppressive and systematic subjugation in all areas of activity, while denying they are doing it. Then they reprimand and punish Black people for *reacting* to white supremacist oppression.

This is a common Gaslighting tactic. Gaslighting is a form of manipulation that occurs in abusive relationships. It is a covert type of emotional abuse where the bully or abuser makes their target question their judgment and reality. The term is based on the stage play and movie *Gaslight* in which a husband attempts to drive his wife crazy by dimming the lights in their home and, when his wife points out this fact, he denies the lights were dimmed.

White supremacy does the same thing to Black society. White supremacists deliberately set up obstacles and societal booby traps against Black people in all areas of activity, and then they completely deny that they have done this. Black people generally drive themselves crazy, constantly trying to prove racism to white people. The reality is that almost every rational thinking adult white person understands what racism is and how white supremacy works. They learn systematic white supremacy from the actions of their peers and relatives. They also understand the unwritten codes that go along with maintaining this system.

4.Revising History

This deception tactic from white supremacists is very common. They like to rewrite, deny, or omit things from history that will potentially undermine systematic white supremacy. One of the reasons why I started making documentary films was due to the fact that too many people in the dominant society kept misrepresenting Black history. In order to maintain systematic white supremacy, the dominant society has to suppress any historical evidence of significant Black achievements. They have to create a narrative that Black people were always naturally incompetent, primitive, and inferior to Europeans and that if it weren't for white supremacists colonizing and enslaving Black people globally, Black people would never have joined advanced civilization. Black society would still be primitive.

In order to maintain this narrative, historic Black figures and Black societies had to be whitewashed. The dominant society uses the "I'm white and I say so" tactic to claim notable Black people were either white or some non-Black "other". This tactic is very common when discussing ancient Egyptians. It's been proven that the ancient people of Kemet (the original name of Egypt meaning "Land of the Blacks") were Black people, but if white supremacists acknowledged that the creators of that advanced civilization were, in fact, Black people, that would contradict their narrative of innate Black inferiority.

White supremacists had to revise history to theorize that the ancient Egyptians were some sort of obscure, non-Black race. Some white historians have even claimed that the ancient Egyptians were a race of extraterrestrials. There are no limits to the lengths to which white supremacists will go in order to deny that Black people created progressive civilizations.

If the true history of Black people was taught by the dominant society, it would completely contradict the ideology of white supremacy. It would also inspire Black people to do more to dismantle systematic white supremacy.

5. Using Racial Code Words

White supremacists today understand that they cannot be as blatant and open with their anti-Black views as their parents and forefathers. When it comes to addressing or dealing with Black people, they now use a lot of coded language with one another. The purpose of these codes is to maintain plausible deniability that they practice any anti-Black racism in their community. These code words are especially used when white supremacists implement actions and policies that undermine Black people.

Here is a short list of racial code words used by the dominant society. Racial code words are created on a regular basis, so it would prove impossible to try to name them all. Here are some of the most common contemporary racial code words:

Chicago = The Black Community
Liberals = Niggers/Nigger Lovers

Black Lives Matter = All Black People
Thugs = Niggers
Looters = Every Black person during civil unrest or a natural disaster
Race Baiter = Black people who call out white supremacy
Diversity = Using the historic discrimination against Black people, as justification to hire a non-Black/non-Anglo person who still identifies as white
Inclusion = Using the historic discrimination against Black people, as justification to hire white and non-Black people from the LGBT community
Welfare Recipients = Black women
Law and Order = Supporting law enforcement officers who subjugate Black communities
Back The Blue = Supporting law enforcement officers who kill Black people
Low IQ = Black people
Inner City = Black neighborhoods
Gang Member = Any Black male between the ages of 8 and 35

6. Feigned Naïveté

A major tool of deception used by the dominant society is to play dumb about racism and the impact of systematic white supremacy. I got hip to this tactic while on a trip to the Polynesian island of Samoa some years ago. I took my family on a vacation to American Samoa because I wanted to visit a new country. I asked the hotel employees at the resort where we were staying if they could find us a local guide to take us around the island so we could learn more about it. My hotel connected me with a tour guide who happened to be a mid-dle-aged white male.

I was a little thrown off because I was expecting a native Sa-moan to be our tour guide because obviously they would know more about the history, ecology and sociology of Sa-moa. Our white male tour guide actually turned out to be thoroughly knowledgeable about Samoa. He was a walking encyclopedia on the island's ecology and vegetation. He went into great detail discussing all the plants, fruits and animals in the area. He also went into detail about the various laws on the island, and even touched on the island's different ex-port goods and services.

The information and history about Samoa was flowing like a river until I started to ask him about the history of coloniza-tion on the island. Suddenly he claimed that he wasn't well versed on that subject. This immediately threw me off be-cause that's the most important part of the island's history. There was no way he could *not* know that history. I knew the basic history of how the Samoan Islands were colonized by America and Germany. But I also understood that discussing colonization and imperialism means that racism and white supremacy have to be acknowledged as well if one is to have a truthful discussion.

I had to ask myself: was my tour guide deliberately feigning naïveté about the subject? Was he getting on the white su-premacist code of silence where people in the dominant soci-ety go out of their way to refuse to acknowledge the exist-ence of white supremacy? When you acknowledge the exist-ence of racism, people classified as white have two choices -

do something to rectify racism's effects or deflect away from the subject of racism and white supremacy in order to maintain the system covertly.

Many people in the dominant society practice the same routine of feigning naïveté as my tour guide. When Black people march in the streets by the millions, begging for justice, the dominant society pretends not to understand. People from the dominant society are so well versed on so many issues – except when racism or white supremacy come up.

It is almost impossible for an adult white person with a sound mind to not understand what systematic white supremacy is and how it works. When people in the dominant society pretend to be naïve about the existence of systematic white supremacy, this is their way of helping to maintain the system.

7. Time Wasting Trolling

Another deceptive tactic white supremacists use, is to initiate and engage in bad faith arguments with Black people. This tactic is done primarily online on social media, in comment sections and chat rooms. Trolling has become a major staple of white supremacist culture. There are three primary reasons why so many white supremacists engage in this tactic.

First, white supremacists must always keep up the appearance of "winning" against Black people. By nature, many white supremacists are cowardly and inept, which is why they depend on a socialist welfare system of white supremacy. The affirmative action system of white supremacy gives benefits and privileges to those classified as white, and systematically cripples Black society as a collective, because white supremacists cannot compete with Black people equally.

When Black people manage to excel over white supremacists despite the obstacles placed in their way, white supremacists often engage in the online harassment of Black people. In the minds of white supremacists, they imagine that their trolling and online harassment of Black people constitutes a feeble "win" for them. They feel that their constant harassment and trolling is a form of punishment for the Black people they target. Even when they lose an argument or other competitive engagement, they rationalize that at least they can win at trolling. It's important that Black people not put too much energy into interacting with white supremacist trolls. The fact is, they are reduced to trolling in the first place because they have already taken a loss and think trolling is their way out.

The second reason white supremacists have made trolling such a major part of their culture is what I call Bottom Feeder Support. Many lower income white supremacists have literally nothing else to live for except for practicing anti-Black racism as their religion. Upper class white supremacists have always used poor white supremacists as their foot soldiers. The Bottom Feeding white supremacists really has nothing of significance in their lives except the psychic satisfaction of knowing that Black society is systematically treated worse than they are. These Bottom Feeder types generally congregate with other Bottom Feeders on specific websites and in online chat rooms so they can form something of a loser's circle. Their activity mainly involves nonstop posting of anti-Black memes and corny racist jokes. Remember, white supremacists are generally cowards and these Bottom Feeder trolls usually operate anonymously in order to project their racial insecurities and frustrations.

The third reason why white supremacists engage in trolling tactics is because they have a vested interest in diverting Black people's energy. When these trolls see that Black people are getting focused and getting on-code with each other, they have to interject themselves into online discussions in order to waste Black people's time. White supremacists know how to weaponize everything and through trolling they weaponize the practice of wasting people's time. They do this by engaging Black people in never-ending, pointless, bad faith arguments that are intended to frustrate the person they are trolling.

Time Wasting Trolls, or TWT for short, understand that their main objective is to contribute to the maintenance of systematic white supremacy. Their strategy is to use whatever means or access they have to disrupt any constructive conversations Black people might be having in their efforts to dismantle white supremacy. The reasoning of the TWT is that if they can get Black people to focus on their circular, pointless, non-constructive babbling, then Black people won't focus on constructive conversations about how to replace the system of white supremacy with a system of justice.

CHAPTER TEN

Strategies Black People Can Use To Produce Justice

I grew up as an only child. I had siblings on my father's side but most of them grew up in Detroit. I lived in Alabama with my mother, and because she worked, I was often home alone.

When you are an only child and a latchkey kid, you tend to become more adventurous. You don't have any siblings to talk you out of your ideas. Whenever I had an idea, good or bad, I would often just do it. I took on the mentality that I would benefit from the good ideas and good decisions I made, and learn from the bad ones.

As an only child, I was something of a daredevil. I would do stunts like climbing on the roof of our house and doing a flip off it. I would tie ropes to the top of five story parking structures and try to climb down like Batman. I would always do weird and reckless things like that. I was always getting busted up and bruised because of my crazy antics. One time I was running around playing and ran into a pole. I split my head open so badly that when I was taken to the hospital to get stitches, the hospital started to question my mother because they thought I was possibly being abused. Eventually, I learned how to channel that adventurous energy into things that were more constructive and logical.

When it became a trend in the mid-80s, I channeled all my reckless acrobatic energy into breakdancing. I reasoned that instead of doing flips off the top of my house, which most likely would not lead to a constructive outcome, I should try out this other thing. I started mastering my breakdance moves and formed a crew that was pretty thorough. We would win local breakdancing contests around the city, and in some instances we made a little money. This led me to focus even more on doing things that would create a constructive outcome.

At a young age I began to comprehend that being bold does not have to be synonymous with recklessness. I learned how to make bold moves that had constructive purposes. I learned how to assess the problem and take calculated risks. When I was a teen I came to the conclusion that being in Alabama would limit my opportunities. I needed to move to a location with more opportunities and the solution for me was to take a one-way flight from Alabama to Los Angeles. LA was a huge, strange city where I didn't know anyone. I knew I had a long struggle ahead of me, but I was determined to live in an environment where I had more opportunities. I made a calculated assessment of the pros and cons. The cons were: I didn't have any real connections in California and I didn't have any money. The positive thing was I had my youth, so I could better absorb hardships. When you are young, sometimes your mind can handle certain types of rejection and deprivation a little better. When people are older, they usually have more financial responsibilities as well as other people depending on them, so any type of hardship would have a more devastating effect. Certain hardships on people who have more responsibilities may cause them anxiety, because if they run into a financial setback, it could affect their children and other family members. When a person is a young adult, they usually go out into the world with a fresh slate, no children and no major responsibilities like car notes, home mortgages, and so on. Young people are usually more bold with their decisions because the repercussions will generally only impact them.

As an only child, I was able to spend a lot of time alone to think constructively. In many cases, people growing up with a lot of siblings or just a lot of people around them, period, often live in noisy environments in which it can be difficult to think constructively. Black society has been taught that we have to constantly engage in noisy activities. Black people are constantly told that we have to get together with other Black people, and when we do, we have to make a whole lot of noise. We are taught we have to turn the music up and party. When we go to church we are taught we are supposed to sing loudly for hours. White churches are generally very quiet when they worship, but part of Black culture is to wail in church at the top of our lungs.

When groups of Black people get together, we have been programmed to believe it's turn up time. No matter how large or small the crowd is, when Black people get together, we are programmed to believe that we are supposed to start stomping, dancing, cackling and twerking. But other groups generally get together and quietly network. Even in semi-social settings, like Starbucks or other coffee shops or cafes, you will often see groups of white people quietly sitting on their laptops or having meetings.

White supremacists taught Black people during antebellum slavery to make noise when we get in groups. During slavery, Black people gathering in large groups was automatically seen as a threat. Slave owners thought that Black people were planning rebellions (which they often did). Laws were passed in certain states that prohibited Black people from gathering in groups. The only group activity Black people were allowed and which made slave owners feel safe, were festivities and church. And the more noise Black people made at these functions, the more safe the white supremacists felt. If they heard their negroes making a lot of noise, the slave owners understood that the enslaved Black people were most likely not thinking and plotting. In some cases, Black people were cunning enough to incorporate rebel tactics in their singing and dancing. They would disguise their fighting techniques with dancing or use coded language in certain gospel songs.

Generally, many Black people engage in loud behavior because, on a subconscious level, they understand that loud Black people make white society feel comfortable.

White society doesn't even mind so-called rebels as long as they're loud. White society understands that Black people marching around with picket signs and bullhorns, loudly verbalizing their grievances, are basically looking for some form of white acceptance. When Black protesters start getting quiet, that's when they're viewed as a threat. If Black protesters are quiet, that means they are thinking, and when you think, you ultimately come up with solutions to your problems.

In many cases, the only time some Black people engage in deep thought is when they are incarcerated in a quiet cell by themselves. This is why it is imperative for Black people to create time to isolate at certain moments in their lives so they can focus and think. This has to be achieved without forced incarceration by the dominant society, because the solutions developed under the confines of incarceration are less effective because they often cannot be executed.

When I was a youth, struggling to get on my feet and to get myself established in Los Angeles, I often went to the library to plan out my strategies. I had to quickly become a solutions-based thinker because I didn't have the luxury of living off local family members. Many of my peers I was hanging around with at the time would engage in all types of reckless and dangerous behavior because they could easily fall back on their relatives. I had no relatives in Los Angeles. I had no safety net. If I made the wrong decisions, I was ass-out. And when people have no safety net, they tend to make sounder, more logical decisions.

One of the strategies that white supremacists have used against Black society is to make Black people comfortable with their oppression. The dominant society learned centuries ago that if they want to quell any potential rebellion by the Black masses, they have to keep Black people distracted and entertained. When Black people were given time off from working for white people during formal slavery and Jim Crow, they were encouraged to drink and party. This same mentality is encouraged and promoted among Black people today. The corporate white media is constantly promoting drug culture and sexually degenerate culture to Black people. When Black people engage in these types of vices, they are considered to be safe in the eyes of the dominant society. Black people who do not engage in these types of retrogressive behaviors, and use their time to think, strategize and come up with solutions to their problems, are generally viewed as a threat. Black people are instinctively aware of this, so on a subconscious level, many Black people are afraid to involve themselves in think-tank types of activities with other Black people. They don't want to appear to be a threat to the dominant society.

The first strategy that Black people can use to begin to produce justice under the system of white supremacy is to recognize that there are no safe spaces for Black people. Too many Black people have been oblivious, or pretended to be oblivious to, the severity of the system of white supremacy. Ignoring such a dangerous system does not make it go away.

In fact, the more Black people ignore it, the more powerful it becomes.

Many Black people do not like to acknowledge white supremacy because it can be damaging to the ego to admit that you are in a powerless, oppressed state. In response, many Black people try to mask their powerlessness by trying to accumulate material items. We have been taught to equate the ability to purchase *items*, which are generally liabilities, as a form of power. Black people being able to purchase material items is equivalent to a person being allowed to have a large screen television in prison: these things just make a person's captivity appear to be more comfortable.

Fighting for real liberation is uncomfortable because true liberation means a group has to do more work to build and maintain society. Many people opt for a comfortable oppression rather than an uncomfortable liberation. Notice there is a common pattern whenever we see a systematic break down in society due to massive protests or natural disasters. You generally see white people stocking up on guns and ammunition. In the same scenario, Black people are usually seen stocking up on flat screen televisions and sneakers. Gaining access to superficial material items often gives Black people a false sense of power and social equality.

True collective power is the ability to influence the actions, beliefs and conduct of others. Power is also the ability to protect your group from outside threats. In order for Black people to achieve this level of real empowerment, we have to remain focused on solution-based codes of conduct based on the way Black people choose to interact with each other (as well as the way Black people interact with the dominant society). Much of this codification is based on the way individual Black people view themselves.

Let's examine seven solutions Black people can use to counter systematic white supremacy. In the words of Neely Fuller and Dr. Frances Cress Welsing, let's find ways to replace systematic white supremacy with a system of justice.

1. Properly Define The Racism Problem

If you define a problem correctly, the solutions will start to come automatically. This is why white supremacists hate it when Black people focus on them. White supremacists go out of their way to get Black people to focus on everything except white supremacy. They have us focused on political parties, reforming the police, and bickering with Black officials who have been corrupted, and so on. White supremacists have mastered the art of getting Black people to perpetually run around in circles, spinning our wheels, focusing on problems that never get solved because Black people, as a collective, never focus on the common denominator behind all these problems: white supremacy.

Every single problem that Black people have as a group can be traced to white supremacy. Without exception. Non-Black people try to use shaming tactics by telling us to "take personal responsibility" for our collective status. No matter how responsible Black people might be, we still live under the constant threat of white supremacist targeting, sabotage and violence. When we look at crime, unemployment, broken families, miseducation, and so on, all roads lead back to white supremacy. We have to always keep our focus on white supremacy's relationship to any collective problem that we have as Black people.

2. Deal With Racism As A Team

Racism is a group sport. In the words of the great Dr. Claud Anderson, when you refuse to play as a team, you lose by default. A major trick white supremacists have played on Black people is to get us to focus on rugged individualism instead of group cohesiveness. Black people are incentivized by white supremacists to ignore or undermine Black collective codification. Black people are programmed to aspire to be the special token negro among white circles, which gives them the illusion of social equality. This also makes Black people feel that they have some special status outside of Black society.

When a Black person is chosen and elevated by white society, this individual is usually presented as a spokesperson for Black people. In order for this type of Black person to maintain their tokenized status, they understand that they have to do the bidding of their white employers/benefactors. They are required to be off-code with other Black people in order to maintain their position and the Black person essentially becomes a mascot for white supremacy. What must happen is that Black people have to stop sacrificing group empowerment for minute crumbs that only benefit them as individuals. In many instances, the "benefits" aren't even tangible. Black people will often receive symbolic benefits such as social acceptance or public acknowledgement in exchange for practicing the individualism game.

3. Do constructive networking with other like-minded Black People.

Black people often waste valuable time trying to convert people into being woke. When you try to enlighten people who aren't ready, these people will often resent you. When a person is physically asleep and someone wakes them up from a good slumber, they will often wake up irritated because they have been taken out of their comfort zone. This same principle applies to being mentally awakened. There are some people who are mentally comfortable where they are, even under a system of oppression. Just like there are people who are mentally comfortable going in and out of jail, there are people who have chosen to be content with systematic oppression and subjugation. And they like to be in situations surrounded by other people with the same proclivity for subjugation.

The best bet is to surround yourself with people who share your same constructive goals and standards. We are taught that the very essence of what is supposed to be Black culture is non-constructive, even dysfunctional behavior. Black people are often shamed if they do not wish to participate in non-constructive activities. Because of systematic racial dominance, Black people often seek outlets that provide a more festive environment. The problem is that these environments are usually not constructive. This is why the partying and recreational activities that we regularly engage in often lead to aggression and violence.

The reality of white supremacist subjugation is still an ever-present reality, and white supremacy is a social prison system. If a group of prisoners of war are constantly partying while in captivity, eventually that energy is going to turn negative because the festivities cannot change the reality of their circumstances. It merely delays the process of coming up with solutions on how to free themselves from captivity.

It is important to try and associate and network with other Black people focused on solutions to constructively empower themselves and their collective group. Associate yourself in person or online with Black people who are focused on economic or educational opportunities. Go to community events that focus on producing tangibles or justice for Black people. Go to museums, documentary film screenings, empowerment seminars or other events that share constructive educational information for Black people.

It's imperative that we limit overtly recreational activities that do not lead to constructive results.

4. Create An Economic Base

One of the ways white supremacists control Black people is through systematic deprivation. Essential resources and tangibles are deliberately held back from Black people collectively. White supremacists also orchestrate many forms of dissension among Black people to keep us from getting on-code with each other.

The key is for Black people to put petty differences aside and prioritize staying on-code with like-minded Black people. When this is achieved, Black people can then focus on creating and maintaining an economic base. Black people instinctively understand that creating a Black-controlled economy is a profound threat to white supremacy. And, on a subconscious level, this is why so many Black people shun the idea of a Black economic base. The dominant society is threatened by the idea of an empowered Black society and, historically, white supremacist society has treated independent Black societies with hostility and violence. Many Black people secretly fear a backlash by white society if they show any signs of becoming empowered.

The solution to potential hostility and pushback against Black economic empowerment is to create protection units among the people in the community. Which brings us to the next solution.

5. Militarize Your Mind

Every living creature has a God-given right to protect themselves. Black people are the only people on Earth who are taught to respond to the culture of systematic, deadly anti-Black violence with *non-violence*. Black people must understand they too have a God-given right to protect themselves and a right to defend their families by any means necessary.

White supremacy is warfare. Because Black people are perpetually being attacked, they must always be cognizant of this reality. Black people must view any and every activity as a means to empower and protect themselves. The main weapon in war is your *mind*.

A person can have all the guns and grenades in the world, but those weapons don't mean anything if you don't have a militarized mindset. With a militarized mindset, an individual will view *everything* as a means of empowerment or defense. During the Haitian Revolution, Black rebel fighters were outgunned by the white supremacist superpowers. In the initial stages of the revolution, enslaved Black freedom fighters did not have the same advanced artillery as the French, British and Spanish armies they were fighting. But the Haitian rebels had a collective militarized mindset and were able to use everything at their disposal as weapons against their enemies. Haitian rebels used plants that could be made into poisons. They used rocks, machetes and fire as weapons. They used the swamps, high mountains, and other rough parts of the Haitian terrain to their military advantage. They were able to use unconventional guerrilla tactics to ultimately pull off one of the greatest military victories in recorded history. The formerly enslaved Black rebels won the Haitian Revolution because enough of them took on a military mindset, weaponizing everything down to their religion. Many of the rebels tapped back into the ancient spiritual system of vodou. They held religious ceremonies in order to conjure up spiritual gods of war such as Ogun.

When a group of people are on-code with each other and they have a collective militarized mindset, they are able to form protection units. A perfect example of this is white supremacist society. White supremacists are a global minority but they have a collective militarized mindset, and they have protection units in place such as law enforcement, militia groups, the armed services, vigilante groups, and so on, that protect them from outside threats. White supremacists instinctively understand the importance of supporting and maintaining these protection units, which is why the dominant society never does anything to stop police brutality against Black people. To ensure the safety of white society, they believe it is necessary to keep Black society in check. The dominant society requires their protection units to brutalize Black people regularly so as to instill fear into the collective Black consciousness.

It is up to Black people to produce justice. Black people need to create the same codified protection units without engaging in unjust brutality. But Black people must use protection units to defend themselves by all means, and to deter brutality by other groups who may harbor anti-Black hatred.

6. Get Insured

A major issue that Black people face under the system of white supremacy are state sanctioned killings by race soldiers employed in police departments. Not only are these race soldiers and their anti-Black targeting sanctioned by the state, they are also sanctioned by the dominant society in general.

One strategy that Black people can use to deter some of the racially targeted violence by these race soldiers is to organize a mass movement to get life insurance. During antebellum slavery in America, Black people suffered all types of atrocities and violent abuse on the plantations. But, surprisingly, during this period Black people were not being lynched or indiscriminately killed by the general white society. After a federal law was passed in 1808 that prohibited the import of enslaved victims of white supremacy, the Black people who were already enslaved became more valuable. Consequently, there was a massive increase in insurance companies working with with slave owners to insure their enslaved Black people as property (Murphy, 2005; Ryder, 2012).

Because of the value that individual Black people had to the slave owners and the insurance companies that held policies on them, these entities would suffer significant financial losses if a Black person was indiscriminately killed by some random white supremacist. In other words, there was a perverse level of "protection" that Black people had against random violence from the general white public. Insurance companies did not want to pay out claims for enslaved Black people who were arbitrarily killed, and slave owners did not want their valuable human property, who provided the labor that made many of them wealthy, to be arbitrarily killed.

Most lynchings occurred after formal slavery ended. Black people were no longer insured by the slave system, and the white institutions didn't lose anything when a Black person was lynched. In order to affect things in the dominant society, Black people have to stop trying to appeal to morality. People who believe in white supremacy have no real morals. In order to force certain entities within the dominant society to enact change, they have to face losing something.

If Black people today created a nationwide movement to get life insurance, this would make a significant impact. We would have to make sure that the policies would result in large payouts to Black families who are victims of genocidal anti-Black violence from race soldiers employed in police departments. If this happened, insurance companies themselves would start to lobby against the arbitrary violence police are allowed to enact on Black society.

In the 1980s, insurance companies used their economic power to lobby for laws that would make it mandatory for drivers to wear seatbelt (Jones & Bayer, 2007; Kneuper, 1994) . This wasn't done out of a moral obligation to ensure the safety of the public. Insurance companies did not want to keep losing money by paying out policies to car accident victims and their families. Their motivation to "do the right thing" and make sure drivers were safety buckled up was purely financial.

When anti-Black racism results in too many financial losses for the dominant society, that's usually when change occurs.

7. Stay Sober

One major tactic white supremacists have used to maintain dominance over Black people is to use drugs as a weapon against Black society. They also do this with other chemicals and mental impediments as well. After the many uprisings in America in the 1960s , white supremacists came up with insidious tactics to not only physically subdue Black males but to psychologically subdue them as well.

To physically subdue Black males, white supremacists created the prison industrial complex. To psychologically subdue Black males, white supremacists orchestrated a drug culture that would negatively impact Black people and attack Black society from several angles. First, drugs would be used to sedate Black males and curb their aggression in fighting against racist oppression. Second, drugs would get entire urban communities strung out, rendering many people in these areas non-productive. Third, the presence of drugs could be used as a justification to criminalize Black dealers and users, which further fueled the expansion of the jail system.

Chemically debilitating non-white people has always been a tactic of white supremacy. Before contact with the European white supremacist colonizers, the aboriginal people in the Americas would occasionally use mind altering substances for ritualistic and spiritual purposes. When white supremacists began to interact with aboriginal people, they introduced alcohol as a recreational phenomenon. That's when everything started to go downhill for the aboriginal population.

When I travel the world today, in many countries that I visit, I see the dark skinned aboriginal population battling a collective alcohol or drug epidemic. This is true here in the United States as well. Areas designated as "Black" are usually plagued with drug use. Some will argue that the white population has a significant drug epidemic that surpasses the drug epidemic in Black society. This is correct, but the difference is that Black society is already in a crippled state because of systematic racism. When people in white society get hooked on drugs, their society has institutions and systems that will assist them to get back on their feet. That same system protects many of them from being criminalized while addicted to drugs.

Major white entertainers, like Charlie Sheen and Robert Downey Jr., had successful careers and ended up with highly publicized drug addictions. Both these entertainers were welcomed back into Hollywood circles with open arms after they reportedly overcame their addictions.

This is rarely the case for Black entertainers. Once successful Black entertainers end up with major drug addictions, that is usually the end of their careers in Hollywood. Black people as a group do not have the luxury to engage in mind altering addictions. We are in the middle of a global race war. And in war, soldiers must have a clear and sober mind in order to assess their position and come up with strategic ways to be victorious.

SUMMARY

During all my travels and experiences, I have come to the conclusion that it is our duty as Black people to come up with strategies to thwart the system of racial injustice. Passively going along with systematic white supremacy is immoral and it is an insult to the Most High. The God of the universe did not create Black people, who were first on the planet, to be perpetually brutalized and mistreated by white supremacists.

People in the dominant society are not going to voluntarily end systematic white supremacy. There are too many perks and benefits in it for them to want to give up those privileges. Non-Black buffer groups are not going to pose a serious threat to white supremacy because many of them are content with the fact that collectively they aren't treated worse than Black people.

Black people must also stop thinking that the dominant society is going to help them to shift significant power and resources into the hands of Black society. White supremacists have spent the last 500 years creating a system that maldistributed power and resources into their hands. They are not going to relinquish the things they have worked so hard to acquire. It is ultimately up to Black people to replace the system of white supremacy with a system of justice.

This can be done and it will be done. What is missing is the collective *desire* for Black people to do it. Europeans set their tribal differences aside 500 years ago, and got on-code with other European nations in order to conquer the non-white people of the planet. Black people have to get on-code in the same manner to produce justice.

Black people must get out of the fear and denial game when it comes to systematic white supremacist dominance. This unjust system has lasted so long because too many of the victims of racial dominance don't want to acknowledge its reality. We can acknowledge our current situation without accepting it as our fate.

Black people globally are dominated, but not all Black people are defeated. You are only defeated when you accept failure. Many Black people are still resisting global white supremacy. In fact, the most notable Black people throughout history are those who dedicated their lives to resisting systematic white supremacy. People like Harriet Tubman, John Horse, Elijah Muhammed, Dr. Martin Luther King Jr., and many others survive in the historical narrative because they resisted systematic white supremacy.

It is our Cosmic duty to not only eradicate systematic racial injustice, but we must also learn lessons from the experience.

Systematic white supremacy is the most powerful system of dominance in recorded history. We should not endure such a powerful and unjust system for this long without taking major lessons from it.

My conjecture is that one of the main lessons we should take away from global white supremacist domination is to never allow petty differences to escalate to a detrimental level. White supremacists were able to dominate non-white people globally because they put themselves between these non-white groups when they were in-fighting. Allowing outsiders to interfere in family disputes, especially when you are not sure of the outsider's intentions, is usually a recipe for disaster. Looking back at history, Black people allowed tribal squabbles to escalate to the point where in-fighting weakened all the parties involved. White supremacists simply came in and used divide and conquer tactics.

Many people wonder why white society, which represents less than 10% of the global population, is a position where they control and dominate the non-white 90%. The reason is that white society is generally on-code with one another, and they have clarity about their position in society. It is the non-white population who is in a perpetual state of confusion, even denial, about their subjugated position. People who are confused or in denial will always be dominated and controlled by people who have clarity.

You are what you accept. If you accept failure, then you will identify with being defeated. The good news is you can change what you will and will not accept at any given moment. Simply choose what you will focus on in your mind.

Too many times we focus on failure. People keep replaying images and thoughts of failure on the movie screen in their mind. You have to choose to visualize being successful and self-sufficient. Visualize a world where you are not dependent on the white supremacists to provide whatever rations they decide to give you. Visualize yourself networking with other trustworthy Black people who share your same vision and ideology of being collectively self-sufficient.

The path to victory is there. We just have to take it. The path to success and justice is there. We just have to choose it. Once we choose our paths, we choose our identities. What you focus on will be your path. If you focus on failure while simultaneously accepting failure, that will become your identity and you will continue down that path. If you choose to focus on solutions and empowerment, you will continue to find the path of success.

I have made it my life's mission to focus on solutions to replace the system of white supremacy with a system of justice. Because of this, I have chosen to identify as a justice warrior.

My question to you, the reader, is how do you choose to identify yourself and your mission, under this global system of white supremacy?

REFERENCE LIST

Adler, D. (1974). The rhetoric of black and white in Othello. Shakespeare Quarterly, 25(2), 248-257.

Alfani, G., & Murphy, T. E. (2017). Plague and lethal epidemics in the pre-industrial world. the Journal of economic History, 77(1), 314-343.

Behnken, B. D. (2011). Fighting their own battles: Mexican Americans, African Americans, and the struggle for civil rights in Texas. Univ of North Carolina Press.

Benson, M. (2009). Hank Aaron. Infobase Publishing.

Benton, T. H. (1857). Historical and Legal Examination of that Part of the Decision of the Supreme Court of the United States in the Dred Scott Case: Which Declares the Unconstitutionality of the Missouri Compromise Act, and the Self-extension of the Constitution to Territories, Carrying Slavery Along with it: with an Appendix. D. Appleton.

Bloom, J., & Martin, W. E. (2016). 14. International Alliance. In Black against Empire (pp. 309-338). University of California Press.

Borelli, J. (2020). Revolutionary Staten Island: From Colonial Calamities to Reluctant Rebels. Arcadia Publishing.

Braund, K. E. H. (1991). The Creek Indians, Blacks, and Slavery. The Journal of Southern History, 601-636.

Brazelton, B. (2021). On the erasure of Black Indigeneity. Review of Education, Pedagogy, and Cultural Studies, 1-19.

Burke, J. C. (2020). White Discipline, Black Rebellion: A History of American Race Riots from Emancipation to the War on Drugs University of New Hampshire].

Byman, D. (2021). Counterterrorism and Modern White Supremacy. Studies in Conflict & Terrorism, 1-28. https://doi.org/10.1080/1057610X.2021.1956100

Campbell, W. J. (2015). 3. OJ, DNA, and the "Trial of the Century". In 1995 (pp. 79-102). University of California Press.

Casares, A. M., & Delaigue, C. (2013). The evangelization of freed and slave black Africans in Renaissance Spain: Baptism, marriage, and ethnic brotherhoods. History of religions, 52(3), 214-235.

Christopher, M. C. (1981). Granville T. Woods: The Plight of a Black Inventor. Journal of Black Studies, 11(3), 269-276. https://doi.org/10.1177/002193478101100301

Clarke, J. H. (1985). Education for a new reality in the African World. ERIC Clearinghouse.

Coleman, A. L. (2007). "Tell the Court I Love My [Indian] Wife": Interrogating Race and Self-Identity in Loving V. Virginia. In Racializing Justice, Disenfranchising Lives (pp. 159-174). Springer.

Collier, S. (2002). The birth of tango. Duke University Press.

Cooke, B. G. (2018). An Overview of the Impact of Racial Hate and Its Manifestation of Homegrown Terrorism in America. Socio-Economic and Education Factors Impacting American Political Systems: Emerging Research and Opportunities, 29-56.

Coyle, P. E. (1996). " The Customs of our Ancestors": Cora Religious Conversion and Millenarianism, AD 1722-2000. Arizona Anthropologist, 12, 1-30.

Cozmo El. (2016). Mer to Moor: Kemet until Now: The Etymology, Phonology, Semantics and Morphology of the Word Moor (Moor What They Didn't Teach You in Black History Class). CreateSpace Independent Publishing Platform.

Cronon, E. D. (1960). Black Moses: The Story of Marcus Garvey and the Universal Negro Improvement Association. Univ of Wisconsin Press.

Cruz, B. C., & Berson, M. J. (2001). The American melting pot? Miscegenation laws in the United States. OAH Magazine of History, 15(4), 80-84.

Cunningham, A. (Ed.). (2017). The Confederate Flag. Greenhaven Publishing LLC.

Dapena Barba, L. By Women, For Women: Feminist Visions of Utopia in North American Literature (1848-1920).

Dear, W. C. (2014). OJ Is Innocent and I Can Prove It: The Shocking Truth about the Murders of Nicole Brown Simpson and Ron Goldman. Skyhorse.

Debo, A. (1973). And still the waters run: The betrayal of the five civilized tribes (Vol. 287). Princeton University Press.

Demby, G. (2013). The Truth Behind The Lies Of The Original 'Welfare Queen'. NPR. https://www.npr.org/sections/codeswitch/2013/12/20/25 5819681/the-truth-behind-the-lies-of-the-original-welfare-queen

Durham, M. (1996). Preparing for armageddon: Citizen militias, the patriot movement and the Oklahoma city bombing. Terrorism and Political Violence, 8(1), 65-79.

Edwards, J. (1990). Race and Religion in 15th and 16th Century Spain: The" purity of Blood" Laws Revisited. World Union of Jewish Studies

Enoch, J. (2020). The feminist civics lesson of 19: The Musical. Quarterly Journal of Speech, 106(3), 242-252.

Etcheson, N. (2020). "When Women Do Military Duty": The Civil War's Impact on Woman Suffrage. Journal of American History, 107(3), 609-635. https://doi.org/10.1093/jahist/jaaa339

Evans Jr, R. (1962). The economics of American Negro slavery. In Aspects of Labor Economics (pp. 185-256). Princeton University Press.

Fletcher, R. A., & Fletcher, R. (2006). Moorish Spain. Univ of California Press.

Fraser, D. (Ed.). (1980). A history of modern Leeds. Manchester University Press.

Fisher, G. (1996). OJ Simpson Corpus. Stan. L. Rev., 49, 971.

Flowers, R. B. (2001). Murders in the United States: Crimes, killers, and victims of the twentieth century. R. Barri Flowers.

Forbes, J. D. (1993). Africans and Native Americans: The language of race and the evolution of red-black peoples. University of Illinois Press.

Foreman, G. (1989). The Five Civilized Tribes: Cherokee, Chickasaw, Choctaw, Creek, Seminole (Vol. 8). University of Oklahoma Press.

Fouché, R. (2003). Black Inventors in the Age of Segregation: Granville T. Woods, Lewis H. Latimer, and Shelby J. Davidson. JHU Press.

García, M. T. (1989). Mexican Americans: Leadership, ideology, and identity, 1930-1960 (Vol. 36). Yale University Press.

Garst, J. (2002). Chasing John Henry in Alabama and Mississippi. Tributaries: Journal of the Alabama Folklife Association, 5, 92-129.

Gerard, P. (2013). Down the Wild Cape Fear: A River Journey Through the Heart of North Carolina. UNC Press Books.

Gilman, M. E. (2013). The return of the welfare queen. Am. UJ Gender Soc. Pol'y & L., 22, 247.

Glick, T. F. (2005). Islamic and Christian Spain in the early middle ages (Vol. 27). Brill.

Goffart, W. A. (2020). Barbarians and Romans, AD 418-584. Princeton University Press.

Grant, C. (2008). Negro with a hat: The rise and fall of Marcus Garvey. Oxford University Press.

Graves Jr, J. L., & Graves, J. L. (2003). The emperor's new clothes: Biological theories of race at the millennium. Rutgers University Press.

Haney-Lopez, I. (2006). White by law: The legal construction of race. NYU Press.

Helg, A. (1990). Race in Argentina and Cuba, 1880-1930: Theory, policies, and popular reaction. The idea of race in Latin America, 1870-1940, 37-69.

Hershberger, M. (1998). Traveling to Vietnam: American Peace Activists and the War. Syracuse University Press.

Higginbotham, A. L. (1978). In the matter of color: Race and the American legal process. The colonial period (Vol. 608). Oxford University Press.

Hillenbrand, R. (1992). "The ornament of the world": medieval Cordoba as a cultural centre. éditeur non identifié.

Hoffman, B. (1995). "Holy terror": The implications of terrorism motivated by a religious imperative. Studies in Conflict & Terrorism, 18(4), 271-284.

Holley, P. (2014). Ferguson prosecutor says he knew some witnesses were 'clearly not telling the truth.' They tes-

tified anyway. The Washington Post. Retrieved October 23, 2021 from
https://www.washingtonpost.com/news/post-nation/wp/2014/12/20/ferguson-prosecutor-says-he-knew-some-witnesses-were-clearly-not-telling-the-truth-they-testified-anyway/

Hunt, L. W. (2021). The Police Identity Crisis: Hero, Warrior, Guardian, Algorithm. Routledge.

Jacquemet, N., & Yannelis, C. (2012). Indiscriminate discrimination: A correspondence test for ethnic homophily in the Chicago labor market. Labour Economics, 19(6), 824-832.

Jefferson, T. (1832). Notes on the state of Virginia. doi:10.5962/bhl.title.33567

Jones, M. M., & Bayer, R. (2007). Paternalism & its discontents: motorcycle helmet laws, libertarian values, and public health. American Journal of Public Health, 97(2), 208-217. https://doi.org/10.2105/AJPH.2005.083204

Jones, W. P. (2013). The March on Washington: Jobs, freedom, and the forgotten history of civil rights. WW Norton & Company.

Jónsson, M. (2007). The expulsión of the Moriscos from Spain in 1609–1614: The destruction of an Islamic periphery. Journal of Global History, 2(2), 195-212.

Karush, M. B. (2012). Blackness in Argentina: jazz, tango and race before Perón. Past & present, 216(1), 215-245.

Karyagdyyev, S. (2019). Oj Simpson Ronald Goldman Nicole Brown Simpson Murder not Guilty American Justice Innocent. Indian Tiger. Retrieved October 23, 2021 from https://indiantiger.org/oj-simpson-ronald-goldman-nicole-brown-simpson-murder-not-guilty-american-justice-innocent/

King, S. J. (2021). Black Arabs and African migrants: between slavery and racism in North Africa. The Journal of North African Studies, 26(1), 8-50.

Kneuper, R., & Yandle, B. (1994). Auto insurers and the air bag. Journal of Risk and Insurance, 107-116.

Lawrie, P. R. (2013). "Mortality as the Life Story of a People": Frederick L. Hoffman and Actuarial Narratives of African American Extinction, 1896–1915. Canadian Review of American Studies, 43(3), 352-387.

Lawson, T. (2014). The last man: A British genocide in Tasmania. Bloomsbury Publishing.

Little, L. K., & Walsh, D. (2007). Plague and the End of Antiquity: The Pandemic of 541-750. ISIS, 98(4), 891.

Lowery, C. (2016). Un-Civil Media and the Social War: Uninformed Facebook Perspectives of the Civil War. In Un-American Acts (pp. 89-102). Brill Sense.

Madley, B. (2008). From terror to genocide: Britain's Tasmanian penal colony and Australia's history wars. Journal of British Studies, 47(1), 77-106.

Manuel, P., Bilby, K., & Largey, M. (2012). Caribbean currents: Caribbean music from rumba to reggae. Temple University Press.

Marsden, A. False Holocaust Testimony, Holocaust Denial, and Post-Truth Political Culture.

Martínez, M. E. (2008). Genealogical fictions: limpieza de sangre, religion, and gender in colonial Mexico. Stanford University Press.

Matibag, E. (2003). The Great Opening, 1751–1801. In Haitian-Dominican Counterpoint (pp. 51-79). Palgrave Macmillan, New York.

Merrills, A., & Miles, R. (2009). The Vandals (Vol. 18). John Wiley & Sons.

Metz, B. (1986). The Cultural Significance of Religious Festivals of Seville: Holy Week and the Romeria of Rocio.

Moore, R. B. (1992). The name" Negro": Its origin and evil use. Black Classic Press.

Mordechai, L., Eisenberg, M., Newfield, T. P., Izdebski, A., Kay, J. E., & Poinar, H. (2019). The Justinianic Plague: an inconsequential pandemic? Proceedings of the National Academy of Sciences, 116(51), 25546-25554. https://doi.org/10.1073/pnas.1903797116

Muller, T. (1994). Immigrants and the American city. NYU Press.

Murphy, S. A. (2005). Securing human property: Slavery, life insurance, and industrialization in the upper south. Journal of the Early Republic, 25(4), 615-652.

Nayler, M. (2017). Córdoba: Medieval Europe's Greatest City. The Culture Trip. https://theculturetrip.com/europe/spain/articles/cordoba-medieval-europes-greatest-city/

Ngai, M. M. (1999). The architecture of race in American immigration law: A reexamination of the Immigration

Act of 1924. The Journal of American History, 86(1), 67-92.

Oliver, D. L. (1989). Oceania: the native cultures of Australia and the Pacific Islands (Vol. 1). University of Hawaii Press.

Otis, D. S. (2014). The Dawes Act and the allotment of Indian lands (Vol. 123). University of Oklahoma Press.

Patsides, N. (2005). Marcus Garvey, race idealism and his vision of Jamaican self-government. Caribbean quarterly, 51(1), 37-52.

Pascoe, P. (2009). What comes naturally: Miscegenation law and the making of race in America. Oxford University Press on Demand.

Pereira, I. (2014). Intercultural exodus. E-Revista de Estudos Interculturais do CEI, 2.

Perkins, L. M. (1981). Black Feminism and.

Pizzo, D. (2007). "To devour the land of Mkwawa": Colonial violence and the German-Hehe War in East Africa c. 1884–1914. The University of North Carolina at Chapel Hill.

Pryor, E. S. (2016). The etymology of nigger: resistance, language, and the politics of freedom in the Antebellum North. Journal of the Early Republic, 36(2), 203-245. http://doi.org/10.1353/jer.2016.0028

Quadagno, J. S. (1994). The color of welfare: How racism undermined the war on poverty. Oxford University Press.

Rath, R. C. (2001). Drums and Power: Ways of Creolizing Music in Coastal South Carolina and Georgia, 1730–1790. Creolization in the Americas, ed. Steven G. Reinhardt and David Buisseret (College Station, 2000).

Rau, H., Buchanan, K. S., Dixon, M. L., & Goff, P. A. (2021). State Regulation of Policing: POST Commissions and Police Accountability. UC Irvine Law Review, 11(5), 1349.

Reed, E. W. (1998). Representations of miscegenation during the Hays Office years: How the public relations efforts of the Motion Picture Producers and Distributors of America helped to institutionalize racism in the first half of the twentieth century. Temple University.

Riches, W. (2017). The civil rights movement: Struggle and resistance. Macmillan International Higher Education.

Romero, L. A. (2021). A history of Argentina in the twentieth century. Penn State University Press.

Ruiz, T. F. (2014). Spanish Society, 1400-1600. Routledge.

Ryder, K. K. (2012). "Permanent property": Slave life insurance in the antebellum Southern United States, 1820–1866. University of Delaware.

Sanghani, R. (2015). The Uncomfortable Truth about Racism and the Suffragettes. The Telegraph. http://www.telegraph.co.uk/women/womens-life/11914757/Racism-and-the-suffragettes-the-uncomfortable-truth.html

Scales-Trent, J. (2001). Racial purity laws in the United States and Nazi Germany: The targeting process. Hum. Rts. Q., 23, 259.

Shaw, D. R. (1999). A study of presidential campaign event effects from 1952 to 1992. The Journal of Politics, 61(2), 387-422.

Spencer, L. (2003). Hank Aaron. The Rosen Publishing Group.

Spyrou, M. A., Tukhbatova, R. I., Feldman, M., Drath, J., Kacki, S., de Heredia, J. B., ... & Krause, J. (2016). Historical Y. pestis genomes reveal the European Black Death as the source of ancient and modern plague pandemics. Cell Host & Microbe, 19(6), 874-881.

Stewart, J. B. (1986). Sts and Black Studies: Partnership for Progress in the 21St Century. Bulletin of Science, Technology & Society, 6(2), 315-318. https://doi.org/10.1177/027046768600600233

Stone, E. W. (2021). Captives of Conquest: Slavery in the Early Modern Spanish Caribbean. University of Pennsylvania Press.

Taylor, R. (2020). Genocide in Van Diemen's Land (Tasmania), 1803-1876.

Teutsch, J. M. (2014). " We Wish to Plead Our Own Cause": Rhetorical Links between Native Americans and African Americans during the 1820s and 1830s. University of Louisiana at Lafayette.

Thomas, T. A. (2016). Elizabeth Cady Stanton and the Feminist Foundations of Family Law. New York University Press.

Turner, M. A., Fix, M., & Struyk, R. J. (1991). Opportunities denied, opportunities diminished: Racial discrimination in hiring. The Urban Insitute.

Warren, L. (2014). Constantine Samuel Rafinesque: a voice in the American wilderness. University Press of Kentucky.

Weiser, B. (1999). Autumn Jackson. The New York Times. Retrieved October 23, 2021 from https://www.nytimes.com/topic/person/autumn-jackson

Westen, P. (2019). Blackmail: A Crime of Paradox and Irony. In The Palgrave Handbook of Applied Ethics and the Criminal Law (pp. 119-144). Palgrave Macmillan, Cham.

Wilderson III, F. B. (2010). Red, white & black. Duke University Press.

Wolff, M. J. (2006). The myth of the actuary: life insurance and Frederick L. Hoffman's race traits and tendencies of the American negro. Public Health Reports, 121(1), 84. http://doi.org/10.1177/003335490612100115

Wolfram, H. (1997). The Roman empire and its germanic peoples. Univ of California Press.

Wright, D. (1974). Leeds politics and the American civil war. Northern History, 9(1), 96-122. https://doi.org/10.1179/nhi.1974.9.1.96

Wright, J. L. (1967). Creek-American Treaty of 1790: Alexander McGillivray and the Diplomacy of the Old Southwest. The Georgia Historical Quarterly, 51(4), 379-400.

Zissu, E. M. (2014). Blood Matters: Five Civilized Tribes and the Search of Unity in the 20th Century. Routledge.

WWW.OFFICIALFBA.COM

Twitter: @tariqnasheed
Instagram: @tariqelite

CPSIA information can be obtained
at www.ICGtesting.com
Printed in the USA
LVHW032114181121
703745LV00004B/61

9 780983 104940